RELIGION AND RELIGIOSITY
IN THE PHILIPPINES
AND INDONESIA

Essays on State, Society, and Public Creeds

Edited by Theodore Friend

Contents

List of Illustrations

Foreword:
One Archipelago,
Two Majority Religions

Theodore Friend

W e think it useful to press questions generally unasked.
This book is composed in that spirit — by scholars,
practitioners, and comparativists, who wish to explore an
unprobed past, to probe an apprehensive future, and to present
their findings to educated laypersons of any culture.

Together we share an interest in religiosity — the
area where religion and politics overlap and interpenetrate.
Religiosity is where no "wall" between church and state can
fully separate the actions of the two; where social dynamics
will elude constitutional restrictions; and where
individuals may feel driven to merge the destinies
of their souls with a path apparently required by the
society.[1] In doing so, both kinds of track may alter.

Such phenomena of religiosity may still be defined as disorders in the Philippines, where there remains a dim tradition from Spain of an ecclesiastical state, in tension with a lively notion from the USA of Jeffersonian separation of realms. In Indonesia, however, pre-Islamic concepts of a god-king merge the realms of state and society. So, powerfully, does the Islamic concept of *umat* — religious community superior to state or nation. In spiritual latitudes affected by the idea of *umat*, religion, religiosity, and right public conduct are difficult to distinguish from each other. Indonesians generously allow that there exist *Umat* Kristen, *Umat* Hindu, and so forth. But to the degree that majoritarian believers, Muslims, in Indonesia act on premises of a prevailing Islamic community, they proceed with views sharply different from and contrastable with the Philippines.

That the two countries differ in these ways, however, does not make them non-comparable. The essence of comparative inquiry, indeed, is the discovery and appreciation of difference. Until now there has been no significant comparative study of religion in Indonesia and the Philippines, or of Islam's effects in the first nation with Catholicism's in the second. We attempt together to open up this vast field of inquiry and speculation for its intrinsic value and interest.[2]

A secondary motivation among some of us may be to avoid seizure of perceptions of Indonesia and the Philippines by the powermasters of American geostrategy, who have defined this area as a second front, after the Middle East, in a poorly defined "War Against Terrorism."[3] In both nations terrorists certainly exist. So may alligators exist in a mangrove swamp. But to take 'gators there as the greatest threat to human health, as against mosquitoes and undrinkable water, would be a major, and stupid, mistake.

---

[1] I mean clearly to distinguish religiosity from piosity, with its implications of insincerity, and from spirituality, with its connotations of solely individual focus. As we use the term, religiosity may be felt by an individual but is expressed publicly in society or polity. Religiosity may exist in the state itself, but, then, in action, it can only be less spiritually earnest and more bureaucratic than the individual variety.

[2] We are gratefully aware of recent publications which plow parts of the field in different ways: Andrew C. Willford and Kenneth M. George, eds., *Spirited Politics: Religion and Public Life in Contemporary Southeast Asia* (Ithaca, NY: Cornell Southeast Asia Program Publications, 2005); Lee Hock Guan, ed., *Civil Society in Southeast Asia* (Singapore: Institute of Southeast Asian Studies, 2004); Virginia Hooker and Amin Saikal, eds., *Islamic Perspectives on the New Millennium* (Singapore: Institute of Southeast Asian Studies, 2004).

[3] Religiosities of various kinds emerge, of course, in such a war. Max Rodenbeck discerns one such "religiosity" in Osama bin Laden's attempt to recodify Islam under his own summoning, with jihad given "the status of worship." "The Truth about Jihad," *The New York Review of Books*, 11 Aug 05, pp. 51-55, quotations, p. 53.

In this short volume, therefore, the essayists — helped by their first critics, the provocative conference audience of April 2004 before whom they presented early thoughts — try to sketch a large human territory together. We can only describe some of its leading religious, social, and political features. We do not propound an action plan. We insist on the basic factual understandings and conceptual traction that must precede strategizing. In Washington, DC, a great city teeming with action papers, we came together to collaborate on think-pieces about relationships among peoples, creeds, and states.

We invite the reader to think of one archipelago (see map, pp. 10-11). Let us call it Phil-Indo. It may be considered to contain one basic ethnicity and one common language family, with a population exceeding 330 million people. If all that populace were one nation, it would be the third largest in the world, after China and India, and before the United States of America.

But it is not one nation. Despite its geographic sameness and common ethno-linguistic features, accidents of history have butchered two nations from it, the republics of the Philippines and Indonesia. And two major religions prevail there. Islam is the census-declared religion of nearly 90% of about 240 million Indonesians. Christianity (mainly Roman Catholic) is census-declared by nearly 90% of nearly 90 million Filipinos. Complications ensue: majority politics and minority resentments, with incomplete assimilations. Unitary visions and definitions produce systematic contradictions, unsuccessful secession movements, and random bloody divisiveness.

We, eight of us[4], assembled to assess these dynamics together; to sort apart and put together as much of this reality as we could in one day's time, assisted by the stimulus of a self-selected audience of more than fifty persons. Our revised essays, and condensed highlights of the discussion they immediately generated, are offered in a spirit of slicing into material that has customarily been enclosed in plastic pouches of one nationality. We are obviously not propounding one thesis. We are offering several different dishes, served on one table. Each writer is a chef who enjoys talking about others' cooking. But the reader, after all, is the diner. He/she will choose according to taste.

As, so to speak, the *maitre d'hôtel*, let me briefly describe our joint menu. David Joel Steinberg takes an overview of the major modern revolutions of Caucasian peoples, and propounds, in contradistinction

---

[4] David Joel Steinberg has contributed a searching essay that serves to open reflection, even though he was unable to be present with the other seven at our gathering on this subject. The Southeast Asia Program/School for Advanced International Studies/Johns Hopkins University sponsored our daylong conference, held 2 April 2004 at the Carnegie Foundation for International Peace, Washington, DC

to current European secularity, the achievement of the Malay world in asserting faith and neutralizing secularism. Following this historic and geographic overview, Azyumardi Azra establishes real religious proportions in present Indonesia, which is distinctly non-Arabic in its mainstream Islamic traditions. He shrinks radical Islam to its real size, and jihadist Islam, diminuendo, still further. He agrees with those Americans whom he modestly calls his teachers, Robert Hefner and Donald Emmerson, that Indonesia will remain an apparent secular republic. But more exactly, a state for believers.

Atheism in Indonesia — none of the writers feel a need to address this obvious point, but the editor should at least touch on it — has been extinguished as a permissible credo because of its association with communism. That party was outlawed in 1966 after perhaps a half-million of its Indonesian activists were murdered, following the events of 30 September 1965. What is borne in the hearts of men may not be inspectable, but carrying any tangible relic of communist conviction is still dangerous in Indonesia.

Robert Hefner describes the latitude of beliefs allowable in Indonesia as a "multi-confessional state." Islam, Catholicism, Protestantism, Buddhism, and Hinduism are all permissible.[5] He observes that within the numerically dominant confession, Islamists remain an "intense minority." Hefner elaborates on the themes of civil religion and public piety which help make Indonesia massively unique among Muslim nations, with its pentagonal permissibility in faith. Pursuing submission to Allah in Indonesia need not involve coercion of believers in other major theistic systems.

---

[5] The problems of state-managed multi-confessional space are shared by post-1990 Russia, with naturally different components. Four religions are generally mentioned there as being of first order priority: Russian Orthodoxy (±75% of believers), Islam (±18%), Buddhism (locally prominent in three regions), and Judaism (largely seen as "emigrated to Israel"). Among the anomalies that arise are that Roman Catholicism is treated as "foreign" (administrative center in Holy See) and Mormons are registered as "Russian," although of American provenance and centering (Salt Lake City).

In this situation, says one acute Russian observer, do not let a spontaneous game of minority interests, or recommendations by American professors, dominate an "unstructured confessional field." [Alexander Olegovich Morozov, ass't ed., Metaphrasis Religious Information Service, "Not Amendments But a New Design," 11 Dec 96, trans., http://www.stetson.edu/~psleeves/realnews/morozoveng1112.html.]

Such concerns apparently animate a recent Russian appellate court judgment upholding a lower court ban, as threatening to Russian society, on Jehovah's Witnesses distributing religious literature. Defendants' lawyers said they will turn to the European Court of Human Rights. [*International Herald Tribune*, 17 June 04, p. 3.]

Donald Emmerson pushes Indonesian religious identity further by invoking contradistinction with the USA. He focuses on the fifth of Sukarno's Pancasila (Five Principles of Nationhood), later transposed to the first, and fixed there as the leading principle. Suharto made the key pillar of national faith become faith itself: "Belief in a Supremely Singular God." This leads Emmerson to speculate on "whither the USA?" He notes that America's pledge of allegiance to the flag only added "under God"[6] in the early years of the Cold War — a phrase driven in by the felt need of some to be more explicitly against atheistic communism. Now, Emmerson senses, "chiliastic Christianity" is gathering speed in the USA. To a possibly overzealous American republic he offers, as a model and caution, Indonesia's restraint in the area of "civic scripture." Here his thought converges with Hefner, who draws attention in group discussion to American evangelism, which has been cantering about in Protestant forms for over a century and a half. Pentecostal self-awareness, with or without Puritan self-denial, is now at fresh gallop in America, and is affecting policy, tone, and votes. In short, it is a force invigorating an always latent and often pronounced American religiosity.

Emmerson is the most concerned about self-congratulatory holiness in the American heartlands. Yet he confines himself, in the end, to noting that state-fostered Islam has diminished in its present likelihood to capture the Indonesian republic. He implies that it was more a threat in 1955, when Muslim parties captured 40% of the vote, or in 1991, when having established ICMI (The Indonesian Association of Muslim Intellectuals), Suharto went on his first haj.

*

Arraying the essayists on the Philippines naturally yields some different themes. The Ateneo de Manila University, where Father Jose Cruz deans, is a distinguished church university which may be considered a higher education analogue of Rektor Azra's Universitas Islam Negeri, although Ateneo is private and much older. Fr. Cruz soberly considers the paths taken by state and church in recent Philippines decades, and the social deficits

---

[6] The Supreme Court of the USA, on Flag Day, 2004, indirectly validated that phrase, exactly fifty years after Congress added the disputed two words to what had been a secular patriotic oath. Doing so, the Court overturned the ruling two years before by a lower court that such a pledge was unconstitutional in public schools.

The decision was expressly reached, however, on the limited ground that the plaintiff parent, an atheist father in a custody fight for his daughter, did not have legal authority to speak for her. Thus the Court "stay[ed] its hand, rather than reach out to resolve a weighty question of federal constitutional law" (Justice John Paul Stevens). [*International Herald Tribune*, 15 June 04, p. A7.]

that have been growing because of the misplaced attentions, or inattention, of both. He concludes with grave and powerful observations about implicit state failure, and the implications of the reality that "the Church is being called upon to bring its vision and its resources to the project of rebuilding the country."

Vicente Rafael proffers a glistening vocabulary with which to grasp Filipino religiosity, which he sees as rising in its political manifestations. Secular expectations, rising simultaneously, are thus far damned to disappointment. Rafael's exercise, in sympathetic identification with fellow Filipinos an ocean away, is discerning on the limits of knowledge and borders of faith; on telecommunications and prayer; on momentary mass identity; on illusions of power, short-circuits of epiphany, and potential for violence.

Joel Rocamora has the unique distinction, modestly worn, of at separate times being unwelcome as a researcher in Indonesia, and unwelcome as an activist in the Philippines. Now that the two dictatorships hostile to him are long gone, he is able to express himself openly on both, and as a comparativist, does so. The weight of his thought tilts strongly against personalism in the Philippine political frame and primordialism in the Indonesian. Philippine experience has made him skeptical of millenarianism, whether of the Catholic or communist variety. His sympathies are clearly with the poor in both countries. He mistrusts "secular sectarianism." He asks sympathy for the importance of religion to the struggles of the poor. And he asks patience on behalf of democracy, usually ragged, always laggard, "precisely because it has to be negotiated."

As we conclude our revisions, the Republic of the Philippines is going through still another constitutional crisis. We attempt neither to track those phenomena, nor those of the Republic of Indonesia, which has come through its presidential election of 2004 with a new stability. We are not trying to body-surf current history. We seek to assess wave patterns in creedal seas and politics, and to appraise great tides in time.

*

To introduce these magnificent seven is a privilege. Before letting them speak for themselves, I am glad to thank those at SAIS who encouraged and supported our conference and its now much refined written product. Fred Brown, then Associate Director of its Southeast Asia Program, has energetically guided, helped edit, and wisely managed us to publication. Chantala Chanthasiri, former Program Coordinator, was an ever-present help. I am grateful to Karl Jackson, Director, for persuading me to visit SAIS, where my responsibilities led to this present publication. Jocelyn Roberts reduced transcripts to texts; Shellie Camp helped as a general production aide; Martin Lasater read proof. Rich and Marcie Pottern provided excellent design. Mary French gave me supportive friendship throughout the project. All of the students in my graduate seminar, *Indonesia and the Philippines: Comparative Development, 1901-2004*, were a friendly inspiration to me. The thoughtful resources of the Starr Foundation have made possible both the conference and its much revised manifestation in writing. We are grateful for their generous vision of that foundation's mission.

Theodore Friend

August 2005

Fig. 1

Graves at Gunung Jati. In Cirebon, Java, a Muslim pilgrimage site dates from the 15th century (C.E.). Islam had begun percolating into Indonesia some centuries before, and by the 15th had increasing effects on morality and aesthetics. (photo by Cathy Forgey)

Fig. 2

18th Century Mosque, Madura. A Middle Eastern Muslim might have difficulty recognizing this as a place of worship by its architecture. But the Hindu Balinese features here reflect proximity to Bali, only 150 miles away, whereas the Arabian peninsula is 5,000 miles distant. (Cathy Forgey)

Fig. 3

18th Century Church, Miagao, Iloilo. The expressive agricultural motifs of the façade reflect Philippine and tropical influence on Hispanic Catholicism, and contrast strongly with exteriors in non-iconic Islam (see fig. 2). This early 20th century photograph is from the National Archives and Records Service, Washington, DC (350-P-4-1-3)

Fig. 4

Nailing of Christ on the Cross. This dramatic interior painting is from another 18th century church, in Laguna, Luzon. (*Art and Culture of the Philippines*, Manila [1975], v. VII) Christianity had only been in the Philippines two centuries by then, but having no systematic religious competitor in the northern and central islands, it deeply penetrated Filipino psychology. The anonymous painter clearly shows a craft identity with the peasant carpenters, as they nail a patient Jesus to the tree on which he will die by Roman imperial and Jewish religious authority.

The Phil-Indo Archipelago

Luzon

★ **Manila**

Philippine Sea

Samar

Cebu

Palawan

Negros

Pacific Ocean

Sulu Sea

Mindanao

Zamboanga **Davao**

Celebes Sea

0	500	500
	KM	Miles

Manado

Strait

Sulawesi (Celebes)

Maluku (Moluccas)

Ambon

Papua (Irian Jaya)

Ujungpandang

Banda Sea

PAPUA NEW GUINEA

mbawa

Flores

TIMOR LORO S'AE

Arafura Sea

Sumba

West Timor

Timor Sea

AUSTRALIA

1

Secularism Neutralized in the Malay World

David Joel Steinberg

The three great, successfully-waged modern revolutions of the Caucasian world — the American, the French and the Russian — consciously sought to circumscribe existing religious authority, positing that religious institutions, beliefs and prior history inhibited secular progress and national transformation. In the United States, the doctrine of separation of church and state has helped to define subsequent American society, giving constitutional lawyers full employment. The Declaration of Independence, the Constitution, and the Bill of Rights have been enshrined as sacred texts; the Ten Commandments, judged to have no place in the court house.

In France and Russia, an even more rigid secularism was introduced through those revolutions, one that still defines contemporary French and Russian societies and cultures. The extraordinary historical power held by clerics, and ecclesiastical wealth in land and control of peasant labor, were deemed to give formal religion inappropriate influence over education, values and attitudes. Organized religion was vilified as reactionary, was dismissed as hostile to progress, and was considered anathema to the shining dream of a new secular nationalism and a transforming world order.

Most other western nation-states, seeking to build their utopias in this world not the next, have also limited in varying degrees their own pre-modern religious institutions and circumscribed time-honored moral authority by demanding that all citizens owe their primary allegiance to their nation, its symbols and its ideology, rather than to any prior religious values or institutional structures.

Not so in the Malay world. Contemporary Malaysia, Indonesia and the Philippines — the three major nation-states of the Malay-speaking region — continue to draw upon religious institutions and authority to shape their several cultures, societies and governmental structures. Despite centuries of western colonialism, the men and women in this important corner of the globe have effectively neutralized western secularism, allowing a much more fluid interpenetration of traditional religious and contemporary secular orders. The capacity to adapt desired elements of westernization while rejecting others is an integral part of an even greater Southeast Asian historical legacy in which Southeast Asian societies have shown an uncanny skill to filter some institutions, values and attitudes for adoption into their cultures even while rejecting others. In effect, Southeastern Asian societies have picked and have chosen some values and institutions from abroad, while managing to slough off others that might seem to outsiders integrally connected with those grafted into the resultant cultural fusion.

It has long seemed reasonable to non-Southeast Asians to suggest a simplistic Hegelian dialectic in which pre-modern Southeast Asian societies sat in a kind of traditional ignorance until colonialism, imperialism, communism, nationalism and modernization (the antithesis) produced a resultant synthesis of secular, modern nation-states. Superficially, newly independent Southeast Asian nations might look and sound like their metropolitan models. In fact, there has been a constant filtration process protecting autochthonous values. The old saw that the Philippines spent 350 years in a convent and 50 years in Hollywood misses the subtle ways that Philippine society has always managed to pick and chose what seemed familiar and comfortable for itself during 400 years of colonialism. Much western baggage was left on the galleon decks of Spain or the aircraft carriers of the United States, even while other metropolitan institutions, values and ideologies were off-loaded into the society.

The folk of Malaysia and Indonesia had become predominately Muslim. The Filipinos became Catholic. But both religious traditions have remained central to nationalism, to modernization, and even to the materialistic development process across the region. Pre-modern religious values and leaders are truly central to the political process, helping to define national identity and to shape the hierarchy of priorities in each contemporary society. The question for scholars, both from within those societies and beyond, is why this should be so and how it happened?

Consider, for example, the latter-day morality play when "People Power" toppled Ferdinand Marcos, restoring democracy to that archipelago. Jaime Cardinal Sin, not Cory Aquino, was the critical actor in that tale. As the Archbishop of Manila and as the ranking Catholic prelate, he mobilized a vast religious and lay network, summoning these women and men to action. Such intervention by a Catholic primate in a temporal power struggle has not been seen in the West since the Renaissance. Sin mobilized the extraordinary resources of his church made militant, used available modern technologies of communication, placed unarmed believers in front of tanks, and thereby transformed a military rebellion, likely otherwise to fail, into a moral and political triumph. Cardinal Sin demonstrated explicitly that he was always the most powerful political figure in the Philippines, had control of the most cohesive organization in the country, and was ultimate protector of the Holy Grail of Philippine nationalist ideals.

This interpenetration of the religious sphere with that of the temporal dates back over many centuries in the Philippines and explains how Spanish Catholic authority, always a tiny minority, controlled the archipelago. It has remained very much at the center of the post-independent Republic of the Philippines until today. And, if there have been deep schisms between a radical group of clerics, organized along basic Christian communities and other social action efforts, and an entrenched hierarchy more embracive of a dominant mestizo culture, all exist under a vast tent of Catholicism. John Paul II, a schooled veteran of the struggle for freedom in Poland, was upholding his European roots when he told 5,000 clergy in Manila on a papal visit in March 1981 that "you are not social or political leaders or officials of a temporal power." And yet, that is exactly what they were, what they had always been.

The Roman Catholic Church has finely honed bureaucratic structures, a compelling hierarchy, and the clerical equivalent of a "democratic centralism" that is more than a millennium old. It has long-established tools to maintain discipline, to define the apostate, and to mobilize global resources when necessary. In Indonesia, on the other hand, there is no similar hierarchical structure or single arbiter of orthodoxy. Islam spread across the archipelago by local choice rather than by an organized and external force. Malay eclecticism has always allowed individuals from different islands, cultures, classes and languages to shape their faith in plural ways. Modern Indonesia is the inheritor of that legacy. Elements of Islamic teaching, traditional values and attitudes suffuse the political, institutional, educational and cultural arenas, among others. It is a truism to note that there are virtually as many ways to practice Islam as there are Muslims across the archipelago. Obviously, there are also many secularists or nationalists who embrace other "isms," including communism and capitalism. There are still others who seek to resist or to reject Islamic influence in the political process of nation building or defining an Indonesian society. And yet the modern dynamic of the Indonesian polity and history suggests that it is impossible that there will soon be any situation in which Islamic elements are separated from either Indonesian culture or nationhood.

"Jihad" and "Crusade" are ancient terms resurrected in this new millennium to describe a clash of cultures and a global struggle, one that has been fought in one way or another for a thousand years from Jerusalem and Constantinople, up to the Danube, across Spain and around the globe to the Malay world. Western social scientists, enamored of their "paradigms," have tended to dismiss traditional religion, its values and structures, as "impediments to modernization." And yet, in both the Philippines and in Indonesia, religious schools and colleges are often among the best. The most transparent, least corrupt secular leaders tend to be men and women of religious piety. All these play a role in attempting to improve Malay societies in this natural world without yielding their deepest convictions about a supernatural world which is prior, preeminent, and prevailing.

Developing countries seemingly need substantially more social cohesion to hold themselves together as societies and as stable nations than the more homogenous, older and economically more prosperous countries of the developed world, because mass compliance of the citizenry may be more difficult to secure, and thus, national unity is otherwise too much dependent on the coercive power of the state. Geography, ethnicity, economic status and social class fragment the Malay republics, challenging the conventional wisdom defining the essential compact mandatory in developing nations.

Each modern Malay nation has struggled to mobilize the energy of its citizenry and, in return, to deliver on the secular promise of modern nationalism, a promise rooted in notions of western materialism. These struggles are a western legacy of the Renaissance, the scientific revolution, the "age of enlightenment" and the political revolutions waged to topple a corrupt old order, the ancien regime. The central ideology of the modern secular nation promises utopia in this world, not the next. The core of the compact between any national elite and the mass of citizens depends on an early delivery of health, education and welfare, on a full lunch-pail and a cornucopia of worldly goods. Ironically, it may prove to be one of the discoveries of this new millennium that the "great society" so coveted by all modern nation-states, including Indonesia, Malaysia and the Philippines, may best be motivated and directed through traditional religious leaders and institutions.

Fig. 5

Japanese Muslim in Occupied Java, 1942. In their so-called "Holy War to Liberate a Billion Asians," Japanese forces conquered the Philippines in six months and Indonesia in ten days. As part of their imperial design, they then waged a "hearts and minds" campaign of propaganda. Here a rare Japanese Muslim, representing religious friendship, is pictured at the Festival of the Birthday of the Prophet; Kwitang, Java, April 1942. [Niels Douwes Dekker; collection of the editor]

Fig. 6

Fil–American Troops Celebrate Mass, 1945. In the battle to take Manila back from the Japanese, all but one, San Agustin, of the twelve historic churches in Intramuros, the "Old City," were destroyed. Tens of thousands of Filipinos died. As the battle ends, a great photographer, Carl Mydans, captures a moment of peace amid the ruins. (Courtesy of the Ramon Magsaysay Award Foundation, Manila)

2

Radical and Mainstream Islam: New Dynamics in Indonesia

Azyumardi Azra

I ndonesia is the largest Muslim nation of the world. Almost 88 percent of the 240 million Indonesians are Muslims. Yet, despite this overwhelming majority, Indonesia is not an Islamic state. Nor is it a secular one, in a strict sense of that term. Indonesia declares itself, and is, a Pancasila state. The national ideology of Pancasila — Five Principles (or Pillars) — avows "belief in One Supreme God" as its very first principle. Globally speaking, Indonesia is unique in this fundamental avowal. Here, Islam dominates the picture demographically, but shares it religiously.

Overwhelmingly, Muslims have accepted Pancasila as the primary ideological basis of the Indonesian state. They feel that Pancasila has been Islamic enough for them, and that it is compatible with Islamic principles. Indeed, many Muslim leaders believe that a Pancasila state is the final form of the Indonesian nation-state. National ideology and the existing form of the Indonesian state go on being discussed, but do not threaten to tear the nation apart.

There have been, nonetheless, certain groups — splinters or fringes — among Muslims since the early years of Indonesian independence (August 17, 1945) who have struggled to establish an Indonesian Islamic state instead. Some of them — like the Darul Islam (DI/Islamic State) and Tentara Islam Indonesia (TII/Indonesian Islamic Army) in the 1950s — resorted to rebellion during the period of President Sukarno. They failed to achieve their aims, not only because the government was able to put an end to their rebellion, but chiefly because they failed to win significant support from the Muslim community.

In the several years since the fall of President Suharto, certain groups of Muslims have made parliamentary attempts to clear the way toward an Islamic state. During four successive annual processes of amending the 1945 Constitution, they struggled to reintroduce the so-called "Jakarta Charter" to its preamble. Reintroduction of the Charter would allow the application of Islamic law (*shari'ah*), which they expected would, in the end, lead to the transformation of Indonesia into an Islamic state. But these peaceful attempts failed. The majority of political and social forces, both within the Majelis Permusyawaratan Rakyat (MPR/Indonesian Consultative Assembly) and in society at large, opposed the move. The pro-*sharia'ah* and pro-Islamic state groups, defeated militarily in the 1950s, were thus kept democratically at bay in the opening years of the 21st century.

Despite the fact that Indonesia is not an Islamic state, there is no question that Islam has been (and will remain) an important factor in Indonesian politics. The sheer number of the Muslim population makes them a target of political manipulation. During President Sukarno's "Old Order," President Suharto's "New Order," and in the recent "Reform Period," Islamic symbols have been used and abused for political purposes. Such practices have intensified recently. A number of parties have adopted Islam as their basis, instead of Pancasila. Although the New Order, in 1985, obligated adoption of Pancasila as the sole basis of all organizations, the matter is again wide open to discussion. The Pancasila — or Islam — debate marks Indonesia as unique among all nations, and among Muslim nations.

Islam and Indonesian Society

Indonesian Islam has a number of distinctive characteristics vis-à-vis Middle Eastern Islam. The Indonesian variety is, by and large, a moderate, accommodating Islam. As the least Arabicized of all Islams, it is much less rigid than Islam in the Middle East.

The American anthropologist Clifford Geertz popularized the term "religion of Java," which he adopted as the title of his acclaimed book published in 1964. The term "religion of Java" refers to Islam in Java — like many other places in Indonesia — as having mixed and amalgamated with indigenous beliefs and socio-cultural tradition. For such reasons, *Newsweek* and *Time* magazine not long ago called Islam in Indonesia "Islam with a smiling face." This Islam is in many ways compatible with modernity, democracy, and pluralism.

Freedom House, New York, in late December 2001, defined Indonesia as one of the "bright spots" of democracy together with other large, minimally Arabicized Muslim countries such as Bangladesh, Nigeria, and Iran. Freedom House found that although there is an obvious deficit of democracy in the Arab Islamic world — "the Arabic core" — democratic ferment is considerable in the countries mentioned above, as well as others with significant Muslim populations such as Albania, Djibouti, the Gambia, Mali, Niger, Senegal, Sierra Leone, and Turkey.

To what underlying factors in Indonesia may this "democratic ferment" be attributed? Two factors stand out: Firstly, the peaceful spread of Islam, described by T.W. Arnold in his classic book, *The Preaching of Islam*, as "penetration pacifique." The spread of Islam was not accomplished by force coming from Arabia, but rather by slow penetration through centuries involving accommodation of local belief and cultures. This process can also be called the "indigenization" or "vernacularization" of Islam. Secondly, the gender structure of Indonesian society, which is very different from the Middle East. While the Islamic Middle East is male-dominated, with women confined to the domestic sphere, Indonesian Islamic society is more flexibly structured, and women enjoy much greater freedom.

The election of Vice President Megawati Sukarnoputri to replace the embattled President Abdurrahman Wahid on July 23, 2001, represents the freedom that women enjoy in Islamic Indonesia. President Megawati gained uncontested support not only from the MPR, but also from the overwhelming majority of Indonesian Muslims. The largest mainstream Muslim organizations such as the Nahdlatul Ulama (NU) and Muhammadiyah — which claim, respectively, memberships of 40 and 35 million followers — did not have any religious grounds of objection to Megawati as a female becoming the president.

Other large regional Muslim organizations in western and eastern Indonesia took similar attitudes on this particular question. Similar positions were also taken by Islamic or Muslim-based parties like the PPP (Partai Persatuan Pembangunan, or United Development Party), PBB (Partai Bulan Bintang, Star and Crescent Party), PK (Partai Keadilan, Justice Party, now Justice and Welfare Party), PKB (Partai Kebangkitan Bangsa, Nation-

Awakening Party), and PAN (Partai Amanat Nasional, National Mandate Party). The PPP, which staunchly had opposed Megawati on religious grounds in the pre- and post-general election of 1999, later accepted Megawati as president. The national chairman of PPP, Hamzah Haz, was elected during the special session of MPR on July 24, 2001, as vice president, creating a duet of leadership that consisted of secular nationalist (Megawati) and religious nationalist (Hamzah Haz).

A limited number of hardline Muslim groups, however, opposed the ascendancy of Megawati on a gender basis. In their literal understanding of Islam, it is not permissible according to Islamic law for a woman to hold the highest leadership in Muslim society and state. These groups, like the Front Pembela Islam (FPI, Islamic Defence Front), Laskar Jihad, Hizb al-Tahrir (Party of Liberation), and Majelis Mujahidin Indonesia (MMI, Indonesian Council of Jihad Fighters), having lost momentum after the impeachment of President Wahid, returned to the forefront in more visible, vocal, and militant ways in the aftermath of terrorists' attacks on the World Trade Center, New York, and the Pentagon, Washington, DC, on September 11, 2001. They subsequently failed to take center stage during the period of imminent US military operations in Iraq, largely because mainstream Muslim leaders had been able to convince the Indonesian public that the US war in Iraq had nothing to do with Islam.

Even though these hardline groups exert only a limited influence among Indonesian Muslims as a whole, they have tried to make use of any possible issue related to Islam and Muslims for their own purposes, including attempts to undermine and challenge President Megawati's authority. Through her term, however, President Megawati survived the challenge of radical political Islam through the support of her office in principle by mainstream Muslims. President Susilo Bambang Yudhoyono, who succeeded her late in 2004, has used similar support to even greater effect.

Radical Groups in Indonesia

Hardliner, militant, radical, or "fundamentalist" Muslims within Indonesian Islam have been given so much media attention in the aftermath of the WTC and Pentagon terrorist attacks that they seem to kidnap the center stage of Indonesian Islam. But they are not new. There were radical groups during the period of both Presidents Sukarno and Suharto that attempted to establish an Islamic state in Indonesia, and to replace Pancasila as the common ideological platform accepted by virtually all Muslim nationalist as well as secular nationalist leaders.

The DI/TII (Darul Islam/Tentera Islam Indonesia, or Islamic State/the Army of Islam in Indonesia) of the 1950s was followed in the 1970s by radical elements like the NII/TII and "Komando Jihad" (Jihad Command) groups, all of which attempted to establish an Islamic state in Indonesia. During the Suharto period, some of these were believed to have been engineered by certain army generals in order to discredit Islam. In any case, all attempts by these radical groups failed, not only because of the Indonesian army's harsh and repressive measures, but also because they failed to gain support from mainstream Muslims.

The fall of President Suharto from his power of more than three decades, followed by political liberalization, brought momentum that allowed a fresh rise of Muslim radical groups. Many of them are new groups, unknown before, such as the Front Komunikasi Ahlu-Sunnah Wal-Jama'ah (FKASWJ) with its better-known paramilitary group, the Laskar Jihad (Jihad Troops); the Front Pembela Islam (Islamic Defense Group); the Majelis Muhahidin Indonesia (Indonesian Council of Jihad Fighters); the Jamaah al-Ikhwan al-Muslimin Indonesia (JAMI); and some other smaller groups.

There is not yet an accurate account of the origin and establishment of these groups, which have made their appearance since the interregnum of President B.J. Habibie. There are reports that circles of their leadership have been close to certain army generals; and some observers assert that their rise has been sponsored, or at least helped, out of conviction or political factors, or both, by certain Indonesian military leaders. It is conspicuously clear, nevertheless, that these groups tend to be led by leaders of Arab — and particularly Yemeni — origin. The leader of FPI is Habib Riziq Shihab; the chief of Laskar Jihad is Ja'far Umar Thalib; the MMI is led by Abu Bakar Ba'asyir; the leader of the Ikhwan al-Muslimin Indonesia is Habib Husen al-Habsyi. All are Yemeni in origin. Each of their groups claims large numbers of members, but it is clear that their membership and influence are actually very limited.

These groups tend to adopt a literal interpretation and understanding of Islam. They furthermore insist that Muslims should practice only what they call "pure" and "pristine" Islam, as practiced by the Prophet Muhammad and his Companions (*Sahabah*, or the *Salaf*). They may therefore be included among the Salafi movements, many of which are nonviolent. But the four groups specified above, based on their literal understanding of Islam and on Salafi activism, have attacked discotheques, bars, and other places they considered as "places of vice." Within this kind of Islamic worldview, they understood the concept of *jihad* as "holy war" against those they consider as enemies of Islam and of Muslims. The generic meaning of *jihad* as "war," however, is only allowed as the last resort to defend Islam and Muslims from hostile enemies. And most Indonesian Muslims do not see themselves in any kind of "last-resort" situation.

In addition to the above-mentioned groups, there are older groups that have been in evidence since Suharto's time. They escaped the New

Order's harsh measures by making adjustments not only politically vis-à-vis the regime, but also religiously vis-à-vis the mainstream Muslims. The most important of such groups is the Hizb al-Tahrir (Party of Liberation), which was originally established in Lebanon by Shaykh Taqi al-Din al-Nabhani, and first introduced to Indonesia in 1972.

The main objectives of the Hizb al-Tahrir are to perpetuate what they regard as the true Islamic way of life globally and, most importantly, to reestablish the *khilafah* (caliphate). This universal Islamic political entity was ended by Mustafa Kemal as he made Turkey a thoroughly secular state in 1922. Some Muslims, however, still believe it to be the most suitable and effective political system by which to achieve Muslim unity. To achieve these goals, the Hizb al-Tahrir resorted to radicalism. It soon became one of the most popular movements among disenfranchised students and young people, not only in the Middle East, but also among Muslim students pursuing their degrees in Western countries.

In the period after the fall of Suharto, the Indonesian Hizb al-Tahrir became more visible and assertive in voicing their ideals. It was very active in mass demonstrations against the subsequent US military operations in Afghanistan. Despite their being more prominent today, their own leader told me that membership in Hizb al-Tahrir has not increased in any significant way.

All the radical groups mentioned above may be assumed to have, in one way or another, theological or organizational connections or both, with groups in the Middle East or elsewhere in the Muslim world. As observed before, the newer groups have a leadership of Middle Eastern origin, and tend to be Middle Eastern-oriented in their ideology and tactics. The older group, the Indonesian Hizb al-Tahrir, in fact, actually originated in the Middle East. Across the band of newer and older groups, however, it is difficult to ascertain any connection with Usamah bin Ladin or al-Qaidah. The leaders of FPI, Laskar Jihad, and JAMI have denied any connection with Usamah or his own base-group. In fact, many Indonesian radical leaders are very critical of Usamah bin Ladin, whom they accuse of being *"Khariji"* (*Khawarij*, or the seceders). Criticizing him as among those Muslims who have seceded from the *ummah* (Muslim nation) is serious indeed, and *prima facie* evidence that they neither have nor wish connections with him.

The increased radicalism of the groups mentioned above is not sparked from abroad, but has a lot to do with the Indonesian government's failure to enforce the law and to solve a number of acute social ills. Continued ethno-religious conflicts, marked increase of crimes, rampant corruption at every level of society, more widespread drug abuse — all have a natural tendency to stimulate radical responses. The abrupt decline of central government authority after Suharto, together with the demoralization of the police force, have become raison d'etre for these "vigilante" groups to take law into their own hands. One important key to solve the rise of radicalism, therefore, is restoring government authority and restrengthening law enforcement agencies.

The pronounced success of Indonesian police in arresting a number of perpetrators of the Bali bombing on October 12, 2002, has forced radical groups to lay low. Some of the perpetrators of the bombing have been sentenced to death. In the meantime, the Laskar Jihad has been disbanded by its leader, Ja'far Umar Talib. Then followed the arrest of a number of leaders of radical groups. Habib Riziq Shihab and Abu Bakar Ba'asyir are two notable cases of those who have been brought to court. How far such prosecutions will proceed toward convictions or punishments will inevitably be a measure both of the weakness/strength of the Indonesian judicial system and the strength/weakness of Muslim political opinion in Indonesia.

Conclusion

With the recent rise of radical groups, the two largest mainstream Muslim organizations — the NU and Muhammadiyah — have voiced their objection to such radical styles. But their voices seem not to have been strong enough, or have tended to be overlooked by mass media, which is more interested in the noise and action of radical groups. Since November 2001, however, the two mainstream organizations have paid more serious attention to the impact of Muslim hardliners upon the image of Indonesian Islam. They admit that the image of Indonesian Islam in particular has worsened following the massive demonstrations against the US in the aftermath of the US military operation in Afghanistan, and after the bombing in Bali (which some perversely, and still falsely, attributed to the CIA).

Leaders of both NU and Muhammadiyah have agreed that they will again project a peaceful image of Islam that protects people of other religions. Their current national leaders, Hasyim Muzadi and Ahmad Syafii Maarif respectively, state that the image of Islam has been politicized by certain radical groups for their own interests, and that such demonstrated radicalism represents political influences, and not a true Islamic way of thinking. Both mainstream organizations therefore intend to carry out a series of activities to tackle extremism through open dialogues, joint programs, and the like. Both also appeal to the Indonesian government to take harsh measures against groups that transgress the law. Syafii warns that should the law enforcers be afraid to take stern measures against radical groups, that itself could pave the way for more and increased radicalism.

With such a strong position at last taken by the mainstream Muslim organizations, it is extremely hard to imagine that Indonesia will become a hotbed of "Talibanism." This is, of course, not to dismiss the possibility of the spreading of further radicalism in Indonesian Islam. As in any other religion, radicalism in one form or another, for one reason or another, will continue to exist among Muslims, including those in Indonesia. But, with the stronger position held by mainstream Muslim organizations, the influence of radical groups can be contained, and will be very limited. Radicals will therefore fail to have any significant impact in changing the characteristically peaceful nature of Indonesian Islam.

The US and Western countries nevertheless should undertake very cautious policies and statements in handling Muslim radicalism in Indonesia. Americans should not overemphasize the threat of such radical groups, because it could give them more publicity, the very thing that they seek. As I make clear from the above, there is not much sympathy among the great majority of Indonesian Muslims toward the radicalism expressed by some of their coreligionists. American overreaction, however, could further ferment uneasiness towards the US among the mainstream Muslims. American alienation of moderate Muslims is really what the radicals are looking for, in order to bring the moderates into their fold. More American overreactions, therefore, contain the potential to give momentum to the radicals for challenging any Indonesian presidency. Their goal, after all, is to create Indonesian political instability in order to bring about a regional Caliphate.

Further strengthening and empowerment of democratic elements among mainstream Indonesian Muslims are the best ways to address such radicalism. It is the responsibility of all Indonesians and friends of Indonesia to try to enhance Indonesian nascent democracy. Given the Muslim numerical majority, this could be done through mainstream Islamic institutions and organizations which have committed themselves to long-term ideals: building Islamic civility, democracy, plurality, and tolerance; knitting peaceful coexistence among various groups; and nourishing respect for human rights.

Fig. 7

Jihadist Warriors Outside Parliament. Two years after Suharto was deposed
from rule after more than three decades, Indonesian religion was in an inflamed
state, and politics was chaotic. Here a privately financed army of zealous
Muslims, the Laskar Jihad, some of whose weapons included samurai swords,
demonstrates outside a parliament in session April, 2000. (Kemal Jufri, IMAJI)
Shortly after, they defied the interdiction of President Wahid (see fig. 30), and
with connivance of sympathetic generals, sailed to Maluku to war against
Christian militias.

Fig. 8

Mosque in Central Jakarta, 2000. A modern *masjid*, in a randomly developed mega-city of more than twelve million people, sits among office buildings, palm trees, and a low-income *kampong*. The red tile roofs of that village quarter are visible left, with still cheaper roofing on the right. (Sidup Damiri, editor's collection)

Fig. 9

Worshippers Leaving Mosque, Central Jakarta. This scene, sociologically characteristic, stands in contrast to the militant protest in fig. 7, which occurred at about the same time. (Sidup Damiri, editor's collection) The largely middle-class worshippers may be seen as performing a *religious* duty, whereas the armed *laskar*, whether out of zeal or for pay, or both, are manifesting *religiosity*.

Fig. 10

Imam and Dukun, mid–1990s. Here in the Kemang section of Jakarta is the smiling face of syncretistic Islam. A Muslim *imam*, religious leader, is pictured in close association with a *dukun*, expert in Javanese culture and mysticism. (Cathy Forgey)

3

A Time to Build, A Time to Tear Down:
Religion, Society, and State in Contemporary Philippines

Jose M. Cruz, S.J.

In some Philippine towns and cities, images of Christ in his passion and death are carried through the streets during Holy Week. The images are ordinarily kept in private homes, either in storage areas or in those parts where people move about such as living rooms. People's sense of ease in having an image of a dead person in one's house is rooted, I suggest, in a practice that dates from before the 16th century. When the datu (community headman) died, his remains, prior to secondary burial, were kept in the house of a powerful family with aspirations of installing the next datu. The ownership of images of the suffering or dead Christ, grounded partly in some ingrained memory of how to deal with a dead headman, is an act of devotion but also serves as an indicator of one's place in the social hierarchy.

Religion shapes society, even while being shaped by it.

The category of religion allows for a fuller understanding of society, but its use is not without risks. The phrase "Muslim Mindanao," for example, prevents an appreciation of the fact that Muslims comprise only 17% of the population of Mindanao and only 4.5% of the national population. It conjures up a Mindanao with a Muslim majority, a notion contrary to fact.

Furthermore, in the phrase "Muslim Mindanao," the modifier is made to stand as a proxy for very complex socio-political realities. The transposition of socio-political realities into religious categories causes a blurring of ethnic and other differences, of contradictions within highly stratified Muslim communities, and of heterodox practices in everyday Islam. Not infrequently, effective remedies elude government planners because categories they employ are inappropriate.

Religion, whose role we seek to examine, does not have a permanent, immutable form. It takes on a particular form, depending on the particular historical period and the particular social context. When that context is pluralistic, contamination can occur. For example, many Filipinos, who believe in the personal God of Christianity, find no inconsistency in believing as well in karma, an impersonal calculus of good and evil that belongs to another religious tradition. A believer, who lives out his religion in a pluralistic context, hears, so to speak, many voices alongside that of his religion. Even as believers formally assent to an orthodoxy, they might be quite comfortable in accepting a variety of heterodox ideas and practices.

The pluralistic context, in which religion is lived, explains how someone can move in and out of belief and unbelief, move from one particular belief to another, and move in and out of particular articulations of one's belief. Since Filipinos live in rapidly changing social conditions, exemplified by the temporary migration of millions, we should expect changes in the forms of religion.

Christianity in contemporary Philippines is in flux, as described above. It certainly penetrates both the private and public spheres. But it falls short of vigorously engaging the space occupied by the formal mechanisms of civil authority.

When the question of religion's impact on society is raised, the People Power Revolutions, EDSA I and EDSA II, are often cited as concrete instances. Undoubtedly, the two events were laden with powerful religious symbolism. However, while religion was involved in the ejection of the incumbents, it did not provide the fresh energy and the new consciousness needed to reconfigure Philippine society. As in the Philippine Revolution of 1898, religion, a century later in 1986 and 2001, played a crucial role in political shifts, but not in any social revolution.

The Philippine society, which religion is supposed to help transform, has had a terrible record of providing for its citizens. In the period between 1960 to the present, the population has grown from 27 million to 82 million, or at an average annual growth rate of about 2.6%. Although poverty incidence has declined from 58% to 33%, 27 million still live below the poverty line, with about 10% of the labor force unemployed. More than 8 million Filipinos now hold jobs overseas, but their increased earnings and the $8 billion dollars they remit annually to the national economy are purchased at a very high social cost to themselves and their families.

How do the masses perceive these social realities, and what has the Church's record been in addressing their social concerns? In 1896, on the eve of the revolution against Spain, brothers Teodoro and Doroteo Pansacula led a successful armed uprising and later declared themselves governor and brigadier-general. When the revolution succeeded in 1898, however, they did not recognize the authority of the revolutionary government led by Aguinaldo and urged their followers to do likewise. Furthermore, they instigated the harassment of the wealthy families in the locality, whose departure they viewed as a necessary step toward the equitable distribution of property. They proposed that the time had finally come "for the rich to be poor and for the poor to become rich." While the elite in various parts of the country considered the expulsion of the Spaniards a sufficient indication that the goals of the revolution had been met, there were those who, like the two brothers, sought freedom from all sources of their oppression, indeed an abundance of all good things.

The incident may be instructive when attempting to make sense of the 2004 electoral popularity, short of victory, of FPJ (Fernando Poe Junior) and of the 1998 electoral victory of Joseph Estrada. Significant differences between them notwithstanding, both appeal to the masses, in the dual sense that the masses relate to them and that they consider the masses their constituency.

Although the Catholic Church has withheld its support from both Estrada and FPJ, Estrada won by a huge margin and FPJ came close to winning in May 2004. When the masses make political choices at variance with the published preferences of the Catholic Church, its capacity to form society has to be reassessed.

The civil disturbances of May 1, 2001, sometimes called EDSA III, are instructive. In the early hours of that day, large crowds originating mainly from the blighted areas of Metro-Manila attacked the presidential palace, in protest over Estrada's ouster and detention. To the chagrin of many Church groups and NGOs that had openly supported the Estrada impeachment, many of the protesters came from areas that had been under their care for years. What the Church groups found disconcerting was not so much the fact that "their people" had moved over to the wrong side, but that the political action completely caught them by surprise. It was as if the Church had been out of touch with its own people.

The May 1, 2001 protest may be an omen of things to come. The event revealed not only a growing desperation among the people, but also their alienation from their traditional leaders, including the Church. If the Church is unable to renew its presence among the masses and to articulate its response to their social concerns, a parting of ways may occur. Millions of Catholics even now take their cue not from Church officials but from leaders like Mike Velarde and other charismatic figures, whose links to the Church are tenuous.

EDSA IV is a distinct possibility. The reason is that, when in EDSA III people went into a rampage, there were at work other players, whose social status and political agenda were not those of the masses. Sadly, EDSA III was never intended to bring about real reforms; nor could that be expected of an EDSA IV of similar character.

The Church may have to rethink its ways, if it wishes to make a significant contribution toward the improvement of the people's quality of life. In the Philippines, Christianity's presence in the public sphere has typically been in a denunciatory mode, not in a constructive mode. The Church has shown itself capable of tearing things down, as it did in the ouster of morally bankrupt administrations. What it has to demonstrate is its capacity to build up, its capacity to sustain a campaign for productivity and equitability.

The lack of articulation of the constructive dimension is indicated by people's idea of what constitutes good works. If one asked an executive to say what good thing he has done lately, he probably would mention a donation made to charity. Other good acts, such as the creation of jobs, would probably not be readily seen by him as a meritorious living out of his religion.

Incredible though it may seem, the average declared annual income of medical doctors in the Philippines is P100,000 or about $2,000. While many doctors carry out medical missions in the slums and perform other useful service to indigent families, the moral sense that impels them to serve others in such admirable ways is somehow suspended in the computation of their taxes. There is obviously a selective application of morality, a situation that arises from the lack of effective Church teaching on social realities, beyond sexuality and family life. Almsgiving has become, for most, the quintessential good work; the reshaping of society, meanwhile, is left to other hands.

As the State shows itself increasingly unable to design and carry out a program of national reconstruction, the Church is called upon to bring its vision and its resources to the project of rebuilding the country. But while its position on family planning is well known, its position on agrarian reform, taxation, the environment, and other important issues is not fully articulated.

The Church cannot hope to bring reform in these areas without wrestling with the formal mechanisms of civil authority. Should it succeed, however, in awakening the considerable qualities and resources of the people, the Church would then have to grapple with the issue of its intervention in matters of State.

Fig. 11

Flagelante (c. 1950). During Holy Week, and culminating in Good Friday, a traditional aspect of Filipino religiosity manifests itself. A penitent man has taken up a cross and borne it all the way from the province of Pampanga to a suburb of Manila. A companion leads him, and from time to time applies lashes to his back. A crowd surrounds the two, with the *flagelante* on the ground. [ALK2, KIT Tropen museum, Amsterdam]

Fig. 12

Monument to "the Philippine Mother" (1950s). In contrast to the different patrilineal systems of the Japanese and the Arabs, family systems in Phil-Indo are bilateral, open, and extended. An important consequence is the relatively high position of Phil-Indo women. The value of maternal power and succor is represented in this sculpture. (WP4, KIT Tropen museum, Amsterdam) The values inherent in this image track easily to the role assumed by Corazon Aquino (fig. 21) after the murder of her husband. This role as "the Mother of Sorrows" was strongly projected on her by Filipino religiosity.

Fig. 13

President Magsaysay as Wedding Sponsor. To serve as a ritual co-parent, *compadre* or *comadre,* is a request that in the Philippines cannot be denied. The role enriches extended family ties with ritual relationships. Here, in the mid-1950s, President Magsaysay is pictured accepting one such responsibility. (Ramon Magsaysay Award Foundation)

Fig. 14

Magsaysay at Giant Eucharistic Mass. The President and his wife join among international dignitaries of the Roman Catholic Church. Attendees flow across the Luneta, a massive assembly space near Manila Bay, as far as the eye can see. (Ramon Magsaysay Award Foundation)

4

State, Society, and Secularity in Contemporary Indonesia

Robert W. Hefner

O ver the past twenty years, public religion in Indonesia has undergone far-reaching changes. The transformations confounded the prognoses of most Western specialists of Indonesia, as well as the master narrative of secularization popular in the social sciences a generation earlier.[1] This chapter aims to provide an overview of these changes, and a sense as to just why they occurred and where things may be going.

Islam in a Pluricentric World

With some 88.7% of its 240 million people professing Islam, Indonesia is the largest Muslim-majority society in the world. It is also one of the most ethnically diverse, with more than three hundred ethnic groups, of which the two largest make up about 56% of the total.[2] Islam first spread to the Indonesian archipelago in the thirteenth century, carried by traders and itinerant holy men rather than conquering Arab armies. Although violence between Muslims and non-Muslims flared in a few regions, the process of Islamization was for the most part peaceful. It left two legacies relevant for understanding religion, state, and society in modern Indonesia.

First, since Islamization was not accompanied by either Arabization or imperial unification, the religious change kept most of the archipelago's ethnic diversity intact. This insured that from early on most, though not all, Muslim Indonesians were accustomed to seeing Islam professed in ways that varied by region, ethnicity, and state.

Second, in partial tension with this first point, there were always Muslims who, notwithstanding the region's diversity, hoped for a more unitary profession of the faith. Religious scholars and traders involved in the traffic linking coastal Indonesia with southern Arabia were especially prone to a more singular and legalistic understanding of the faith. They were also among the first to respond to the reformist currents emanating from the Middle East in the late eighteenth century. Inland societies with established court traditions, like the Javanese and Sundanese, tended to prefer a more indigenized Islam that highlighted Islamic spirituality as much as details of the law. Since the Islamic resurgence of the 1980s, most of these latter groups have become more "normative" in their profession of the faith. Nonetheless, behind the orthodox veil, Muslim Indonesia is still marked by great tension between those who favor a unitary and state-imposed confession of the faith, and those who prefer or advocate pluralistic Islam.

Notwithstanding the efforts of a few secular-modernizers, the mainstream tradition of religious politics in twentieth century Indonesia was never *secular* nationalist in aspiration, contrary to France or Republican Turkey, where nationalism separated religion from the state and restricted religion to private life. The compromise negotiated by Indonesia's founders promoted a *multiconfessional nationalism* that recognized the state's interest in supporting public religion while not establishing a state religion. In this sense, religious politics in Indonesia was always far more civic republican than it was liberal in any Western sense.[3]

In 1955, Muslim parties obtained more than 40% of the vote but failed to win the first national elections as a whole. Over the next ten years their influence diminished further. As the young country slipped into economic crisis, secular-nationalists and socialist parties made headway, not least of all among the poor of Java. In the early 1960s Indonesia had the distinction of having the largest communist party in the non-communist world. During these same years, President Sukarno moved closer to allies in the Communist

Party. Sukarno compounded his leftward tilt by repressing modernist Muslim organizations, actions which were to cause lasting Muslim resentment.

New Order Commands

A military-dominated "New Order" regime came to power in October 1965 in the aftermath of a failed leftist officers' coup. Led by a quiet young general named Suharto, one of the new government's first actions was to ban the Communist Party. It also embarked on an authoritarian program of national development, which was effective at least economically. Suharto opened the country to foreign investment and achieved sustained economic growth. Although during 1965-1966 he had relied on Muslim organizations to help destroy the Communist Party, Suharto quickly distanced himself from those allies and rejected their demands for the implementation of Islamic law. For twenty years of his thirty-two year rule, the President promoted a culturally conservative and politically authoritarian variant of multiconfessional nationalism. But changes in society would eventually make this formula unsustainable.

Although the New Order professed neutrality in dealing with state-sanctioned religions, it meddled extensively in religious affairs. One of the regime's first actions was to ban hundreds of mystical (*kebatinan*) sects regarded as left-wing, or offensive to mainstream Muslims. The government also prohibited public expressions of Chinese religion, as well as the import of literature written in Chinese characters. Chinese Indonesians were encouraged to convert to Buddhism or Christianity.

The government also used the full force of the state to promote the Pancasila ("five principles") as the ideological foundation of the state. Although the first of the Pancasila's principles makes belief in God a tenet of the nation, the principle steers clear of making Islam the religion of state. Conservative Muslims resented both the Pancasila and the heavy-handed way it was forced on their organizations. The impact of Pancasila policies on Muslim groupings was minor, however, by comparison with its effect on the ethnic and local religions practiced by hinterland minorities in Kalimantan, Sulawesi, and eastern Indonesia. The policy was equally disastrous for Javanese "new religions," such as Permai and the Buda-Vishnu religion, syncretic movements which had gained a small but vocal following in the period from 1920 to 1965.[4]

In one swipe, the New Order banned all of these religions. In their place, the state required citizens to profess one among five state-recognized religions: Islam, Protestantism, Catholicism, Hinduism, and Buddhism. Even the adherents of these religions were subject to new state regulations, such as the requirement that all religions, including Hinduism and

Buddhism, be monotheistic. Notwithstanding these interventions, the New Order government remained even-handed in its treatment of the five state-sanctioned faiths. This equity of attention was to change in the final years of the Suharto regime.

Beginning in the late 1970s, Indonesia was swept by an Islamic resurgence, similar in social form if not political temperament to those experienced a decade earlier in the Muslim Middle East and South Asia. The indices of the Indonesian resurgence were growing mosque attendance, enrollment in religious classes, the adoption of Islamic dress (including the wearing of the veil by women), and the expansion of Muslim educational and social organizations. Although there were a few extremists at its fringe, the mainstream of the resurgence was never politically radical. Its primary social impulse was pietistic and public-ethical, aimed at heightening the role of Islam in social life. Nor was the resurgence a mere product of New Order engineering. Indeed, if anything, the resurgence represented an assertion of religious society *against* the state. It also spelled trouble for the Suharto government's policies on nation and religion.

Pressures soon mounted for the government to make greater concessions to Muslim interests. Responding to the changed environment, in the late 1980s Suharto broke with his separate-but-equal policy and began to extend greater aid to the Muslim community.[5] He lifted the ban on the veil in state schools, and imposed tighter restrictions on the activities of Christian missionaries. Suharto also increased state subsidies for mosque building, Islamic education, Muslim television programming, the celebration of religious holidays, and preferential treatment for Muslim entrepreneurs in state contracts. For the first time, too, and with the help of his volatile son-in-law, Prabowo Subianto, the President also sponsored an Islamist faction in the armed forces, previously a bastion of conservative secular nationalism.

During the last ten years of his rule, President Suharto also tried to co-opt the mainstream leadership of the country's two largest Islamic organizations, the Nahdlatul Ulama (which today has an estimated 40 million supporters) and the Muhammadiyah (35 million). Established in the early years of the twentieth century (1926 and 1912, respectively), these two have become the world's largest mass-based Muslim social organizations. Since their founding, both groups have prided themselves on their independence, as well as their prioritizing of education and social welfare over politics. This legacy has long distinguished Indonesian Islam from most Middle Eastern countries. It has also provided a solid foundation for a Muslim civil society.

In the early 1990s, the leadership of both the NU and Muhammadiyah agreed to cooperate with President Suharto on social and educational initiatives. Much to the President's consternation, however, they also continued to press for democratic reform. Faced with this challenge, in the mid-1990s President Suharto changed political tack. Rather than continuing his outreach to moderate Muslims, Suharto reached out to hardline groups like KISDI and the Dewan Dakwah Islamiyah Indonesia, both of which had a reputation for being fiercely anti-Western and anti-Christian. Viewed in terms of his own political aims, the President's efforts failed. With the onset of the Asian economic crisis in late 1997, support for the Suharto regime waned, and the President was forced from power in May 1998. Sadly, the months leading up to his resignation were marked by anti-Chinese and anti-Christian riots, some of which showed the tell-tale signs of regime provocation.

Unfortunately, this habit of sectarian trawling — using or even worsening religious tensions to boost one's own political support — did not end with Suharto's resignation. After May 1998, some politicians and ethnic leaders appealed to ethnoreligious sentiments as well. The tactic had an especially bloody consequence in Maluku, Central Kalimantan, and South Sulawesi, where Christians and Muslims are roughly equal in numbers. Sectarian paramilitaries soon sprouted across these troubled regions. The paramilitarism wasn't just a Muslim problem. In the province of Central Kalimantan local Christians launched brutal campaigns of ethnic cleansing, slaughtering hundreds of Madurese Muslims. In Central Sulawesi, Christian and Muslim gangs alike carried out atrocities. In Maluku, too, Christian and Muslim paramilitaries battled each other, leaving 9,000 dead and 900,000 homeless.[6]

In the nation's capital, too, a few politicians in the early post-Suharto years lent their support to hardline Islamist groupings like the Laskar Jihad and the Islamic Defenders Front. Research conducted by the Brussels-based International Crisis Group has shown that some of this support was intended to destabilize the Wahid administration (which governed from October 1999 to July 2001) and to undercut its programs of democratic reform. Since the Bali bombings in October 2002, however, elite patronage of radical Islamist paramilitaries has diminished significantly.[7]

Intense Minorities and the Political Future

Notwithstanding the turbulence of the early post-Suharto period, the majority of Indonesian Muslims remain moderate in their views on Islam and politics. The national assembly has recently twice rebuffed efforts to implement *shari'a*. Surveys have shown that the majority of Muslims see their religion as compatible with democracy and human rights. The elections of June 1999 were a triumph of moderation, with Islamists winning only 16% of the vote. Despite a sharp uptick in anti-Americanism in the aftermath of the U.S. interventions in Afghanistan and Iraq, the elections of April 2004 yielded similar results, with moderate Muslims and nationalist parties winning the lion's share of the vote. Even the Islamist Justice and Welfare Party (*Partai Keadilan Sejahtera*) campaigned on an anti-corruption platform, downplaying its commitment to the implementation of Islamic law.[8]

While rejecting religious extremism, most Muslims seem uncomfortable with the idea that the state should have nothing to do with religion. A French- or American-style separation of religion and state has some support in Christian circles, but not among Muslims. In practice if not explicit principle, then, the policies of the state remain premised on a multiconfessional nationalism. As during the late Suharto period, Islam continues to receive a share of state funding for religion greater than the already great proportion of Muslims in society.

Since the late Suharto era, however, practitioners of non-Muslim religions now enjoy a greater measure of freedom — at least when it comes to managing their own affairs. A striking indication of the new freedom is that Confucianism is now recognized as an official option for ethnic Chinese.[9] Among urban Hindus, Chinese, and some Protestant Christians, we have even begun to see a pattern of fluid and voluntaristic affiliation (and affiliation switching) not unlike that Susan Ackerman and Raymond Lee reported for non-Muslim Malaysians in the late 1980s.[10] However, consistent with a pattern that emerged in the final years of the New Order, this new freedom does *not* extend to relations with Muslims. However modest their electoral gains, conservative Muslims have continued to press for legal restrictions on the rights of non-Muslims to erect houses of worship, marry Muslims without first converting to Islam, or otherwise bring their religion into the public sphere. Examples like these remind one of the old adage in introductory political science that policy is shaped by intense minorities more than it is shaped by majorities. For some time to come, conservative Islamic opposition to liberal policies is going to exercise a significant influence, from an intense minority, on inter-religious relations.

In partial tension with this last point, the leadership of the mainstream Muslim community seems more determined than ever to guard against extremist provocation in the name of Islam. NU and Muhammadiyah have together launched numerous programs in support of civic peace and moderation. Under the rectorship of Professor Azyumardi Azra, the State Islamic University in Jakarta has pioneered impressive programs of civic education in Muslim institutions of higher learning. The Yogyakarta Muhammadiyah University has implemented programs of a similar nature, differing from the UIN effort only in their greater attention to Muhammadiyah history.[11]

Indonesia's post-Suharto troubles are far from over. The moderation of the Muslim majority still faces three looming challenges. First, as recent surveys of foreign investors remind us, the government remains one of the most corrupt in Asia. The reluctance of authorities to tackle corruption fuels popular skepticism toward the political and legal system as a whole, and buttresses Islamist calls for the implementation of Islamic law. However undemocratic many of its historical provisions, part of *shari`a*'s appeal always has lain in a quasi-democratic impulse: that no person should be above the law, and that the only law that is above everyone is God's.[12] Seen in this light, it is not at all surprising that some Muslims would respond to crime and corruption with calls for *shari`a*.

Second, in the aftermath of the Bali bombings, the largest Islamist paramilitaries have scaled back their activities. But some armed groups still would like to use the state to impose their views. These militias now operate in the shadows of mainstream Muslim society. In the early post-Suharto period, these groups were able to exercise an influence far greater than their numbers in society because of bitter ethnoreligious tensions, the breakdown of state administration, and patronage of select militias by disaffected members of the political and military establishment. These influences have diminished as the post-Suharto era has stabilized.

Unfortunately, an independent *jihadi* fringe continues to operate, using violence like that of the Bali bombings in October 2002 to promote its cause. The *jihadis* may be few in number, but they have made skillful use of global political crises like the war in Iraq, which has done untold damage to America's image as a promoter of democracy and the rule of law. Here again, intense minorities, even small ones, can exercise significant influence when state and society lack the will or resources to dampen their enthusiasms. Although unlikely to destabilize the country in any pivotal way, Muslim radicals will remain players on the Indonesian scene, as they always have, and may again attempt acts objectionable to the mainstream of the Muslim community.

A third and equally serious challenge to Indonesian Islam's moderate traditions is that in a few provinces radical Islamists, having put armed struggle aside for the moment, are escalating their threats against Muslim liberals, unveiled women, religious minorities, and other "enemies of Islam." The phrase one hears in Indonesia these days is that the radicals have adopted a strategy of *horizontal* mobilization in place of their earlier *vertical* tactics. In districts like Tasikmalaya, West Java and Makassar, South Sulawesi, local groups are concentrating their energies on pressuring local legislatures to implement Islamic law. Although for the moment these campaigns appear to have stalled, they may reappear, for horizontal radicalism is a preferred tactic of impatient believers.

Indonesia has never embraced and will not embrace a French or American separation of religion and state. Even in the Sukarno era, the state conceded the Muslim point that it is in the interest of both state and society to promote religion. In fact, with the notable exception of Turkey,[13] most modern Muslim nations have adopted variants of this same orientation. Western liberals who may find offensive the policies that are corollary to this point of view may wish to remember that, for most of the modern era, the French and American separation of religion and state was the exception rather than the rule in the West. Although there is no single pattern, tax subsidies to Christian organizations and religious instruction in state schools were common in most of Western Europe until the middle of the twentieth century. In several Western European democracies, they are the operative rule still today.[14]

The Indonesian situation is distinctive, then, less with regard to the concessions the state makes to public religion than it is in the fact that the majority of Muslims continue to interpret this charge in a moderate manner. To judge by a voting pattern across half a century, most are comfortable with state promotion of religion but not with the formal establishment of an Islamic state. Most also seem to believe that the state's promotion of religion must not allow the government a monopoly over religious expression.

The Islamic resurgence that has transformed public religion in Indonesia across the past twenty years does not, then, mean the country is about to witness a radical Islamist ascent. Cultural globalization and international conflicts like the war in Iraq have given internationalist *jihadism* a new lease on life, but Muslim politics in Indonesia remains as diverse as ever. Indeed, the *jihadis* present such an awful threat to ordinary Muslims that, notwithstanding their ability to wreak havoc, they are unlikely to receive broad public support any time soon.

The more pervasive impact of the Islamic resurgence has been not a unitary and dominant radicalism, then, but the fact that Islamic issues figure prominently in public policy debates. This will likely remain the pattern for years to come. For the time being, there is no going back to the conceit of 1950s' secularization theory, with its assumption that, where democracy prevails, it will do so on the basis of religion's decline. The United States and some other portions of the Western world never really conformed to the "grand narrative" of secularization theory, with its predictions of religion's privatization and eventual decline.[15] Why should Indonesia and the rest of the Muslim world ever do so?

Indonesia is not about to descend into an Islamist maelstrom. But the course of Muslim politics could yet go in any of several directions, some democratic, others not. Since a public and political Islam is there to stay, one of the most pressing challenges for Muslim moderates will be to contain the fervor of the "intense" Islamist minority, by channeling the broader community's energies away from radicalism and into democratic institutions. The outcome of the moderates' efforts to demonstrate the compatibility of Islam and democracy will be pivotal to the future of both the Muslim community and Indonesian politics.

As with ethnoreligious pluralism in the West, getting the democratic message out and making it politically effective are not easy matters. But what makes Indonesia unique among Muslim nations is that, despite the chaos of recent years, much of the framework for a civil Islam remains intact within a multiconfessional republic. If and when the country's leaders can devise state institutions capable of working with rather than against pluralist groupings in society, Indonesia's religious future may shine again to its own peoples, and even as a model to others.

Fig. 15

Dutch Universal Church and Cemetery. In a late imperial act, the Netherlands conveyed its Western universalism with a worship site and holy ground in Jakarta for Christians, Jews, and Muslims. (Cathy Forgey) But the Dutch concept was made parochial and had already been bypassed by Sukarno's revolutionary speech on Pancasila (June, 1945). The new republic would recognize five religions: Islam, Catholicism and Protestantism (treated separately as *Katolik* and *Kristen*), Buddhism, and Hinduism.

Fig. 16

Chinese Indonesian at Buddhist Altar. Chinese Indonesians, if they were Buddhist, had a clear means of religious expression, as shown here about 1950. [Niels Douwes Dekker, collection of the editor] If they were unaffiliated, President Suharto's dictates of the late 1960s drove many to locate themselves as Christians for security. Those Chinese who see themselves as Confucian in ritual or religion still have no secure formal recognition, but President Wahid in 2000 removed barriers to their public worship.

Fig. 17

Protestant Church, North Sulawesi, 1997. This outlying church in Manado may typify much provincial Christianity. Note resources put into the façade, compared with rusting roof. [Byron Black] In Poso (in adjoining Central Sulawesi), demographic and religious tensions between previously peaceful Christians and Muslims led to episodic fighting until a peace accord was reached in December 2001. Deaths, mostly among Muslims, were estimated at between 1,000 and 2,500.

Fig. 18

Hindu Funeral Pyre, Bali, 2000. The prominent immigrant artist, Antonio Blanco (1927-2000), was a Filipino of Catalan descent, born in Manila and trained in New York City. His cremation in Ubud was at one level a tourist event. At deeper levels, however, his funeral was a dramatic expression of Hindu traditions in Bali. (Kemal Jufri, IMAJI)

NOTES

1 On secularization theory as a master narrative, see Jeffrey Cox, "Master narratives of long-term religious change." In Hugh McLeod and Werner Ustorf, *The Decline of Christendom in Western Europe, 1750-2000* (Cambridge: Cambridge University Press, 2003), pp. 201-217.

2 See Leo Suryadinata, Evi Nurvidya Arifin, and Aris Ananta, *Indonesia's Population: Ethnicity and Religion in a Changing Political Landscape* (Singapore: Institute of Southeast Asian Studies, 2003).

3 On civic republican democracy, see Frank Cunningham, *Theories of Democracy: A Critical Introduction* (New York: Routledge, 2002), pp. 53-59.

4 On Permai, see Clifford Geertz, *Religion of Java* (Glencoe, IL: Free Press, 1960); on the Buda-Vishnu religion, see Robert W. Hefner, "Islamizing Java? Religion and Politics in Rural East Java," *The Journal of Asian Studies* 3:46 (1987), pp. 533-554.

5 See Robert W. Hefner, *Civil Islam: Muslims and Democratization in Indonesia* (Princeton, NJ: Princeton University Press, 2000).

6 See Human Rights Watch, "Breakdown: Four Years of Communal Violence in Central Sulawesi" (New York: Human Rights Watch Papers, Vol. 14, No. 9C, 2002); and International Crisis Group, "Communal Violence in Indonesia: Lessons from Kalimantan" (Brussels: ICG Asia Report No. 19, 2001).

7 See Robert W. Hefner, "Muslim Democrats and Islamist Violence in Post-Suharto Indonesia." In Robert W. Hefner, ed., *Remaking Muslim Politics: Pluralism, Contestation, Democratization* (Princeton, NJ: Princeton University Press, 2004).

8 This point was eloquently raised by Dr. Azyumardi Azra of the National Islamic University at the April 2, 2004 conference at which the present paper was first discussed.

9 As one more sign of the less Jakarta-centric nature of politics in the post-Suharto era, however, government officials in some localities have reportedly refused to implement this policy, not allowing local Chinese to register as Confucian.

10 See Susan E. Ackerman and Raymond L. M. Lee, *Heaven in Transition: Non-Muslim Religious Innovation and Ethnic Identity in Malaysia* (Honolulu: University of Hawaii Press, 1988), pp. 155-162.

11 The texts for these programs bear remarkable testimony to the intellectual sophistication of Indonesia's Muslim democrats. See Abdul Rozak, Wahdi Sayuti, and Andi Syafrani, eds., *Pendidikan Kewargaaan: Demokrasi, Hak Asasi Manusia, dan Masyarakat Madani* [Citizen Education: Democracy, Human Rights, and Civil Society] (Jakarta: Hidayatullah National Islamic University, 2003); and Asykuri ibn Chamim, ed., *Pendidikan Kewarganegaraan: Menuju Kehidupan yang Demokratis dan Berkeabadan* [Citizenship Education: Toward a Democratic and Civil Life] (Yogyakarta: Kantor Majelis Pendidikan Tinggi, Pimpinan Pusat Muhammadiyah, 2003).

12 On the law and democracy, see Khaled Abou El Fadl, *Islam and the Challenge of Democracy* (Princeton, NJ: Princeton University Press, 2004), pp. 7-10.

[13] On Turkey's unusual legacy of secular nationalism, see Niyazi Berkes, *The Development of Secularism in Turkey* (New York: Routledge, 1998).

[14] See Hugh McLeod, "Introduction." In McLeod, ed., *The Decline of Christendom in Western Europe, 1750-2000* (Cambridge: Cambridge University Press, 2003), pp. 1-26; and Stephen V. Monsma and J. Christopher Soper, *The Challenge of Pluralism: Church and State in Five Democracies* (Lanham, MD: Rowman & Littlefield, 1997).

[15] For a forceful analysis of how Americans never conformed to secularization theory, see Roger Finke and Rodney Stark, *The Churching of America 1776-1990: Winners and Losers in our Religious Economy* (New Brunswick, NJ: Rutgers University Press, 1992).

5

Spectral Communities: Religiosity and Nationhood in the Contemporary Philippines

Vicente L. Rafael

From Monday to Friday between 5-6 pm, a minor miracle takes place at my home in Seattle. The tabloid show, "TV Patrol," is broadcast via satellite and cable from Manila to my part of the Pacific Northwest in the US. The image of well-known personality Corina Sanchez suddenly appears on my television set, the sound of her voice filling the room, bringing stories and images of current events in the Philippines. This is in some ways nothing short of miraculous. That which is distant instantaneously comes close, and that which is absent magically becomes present. Yet, this sudden proximity does not dissolve the great gulf that separates me from the Philippines, but rather amplifies it further. This presence of images and voices does not bring to my home, for example, the faces of politicians, the streets of the city, the suspected thief apprehended by the police. Instead, they keep such people and things at bay.

Thanks to the media of television and the mediation of "TV Patrol," the Philippines is there by not being there. It comes to me as a kind of spectral nation. Whenever I turn on the television, I welcome without always intending to and without comprehending how, these ghosts — the spirits of the nation emanating from my original home into my present one. In doing so, I take for granted the largely mysterious but unseen processes that make such transmissions possible: the satellite feeds, the computer software and electric impulses that carry waves of sound and bits of visual data, as well as the tangled political economy of private ownership, government regulation, media conglomerates, and so forth. Even if I were to become aware of the workings of these technologies and political economies, I would have to set them aside momentarily in order to see and hear what comes before me. I cannot see what enables me to see: the invisible and secret operations, the arcane codes, the endless calculations that power the transmission of this spectral nation. Yet, along with more than two and a half million Filipinos in the United States, I find myself addressed by that which remains steeped in secrecy. Simultaneously intimate and exterior to me, it calls me to become part of a virtual public sphere. I heed this call to the extent that I believe in what it says, because, first and foremost, it speaks in the national language, Filipino. Unlike anything else on my television set, "TV Patrol" is the only program at this hour broadcast in this language. By watching it, I believe its fundamental message: this is for you, right now, you out there who understand this language and are therefore part of the community of Filipinos everywhere in the world. Even if I am skeptical about the facts and suspicious of the ways it frames or interprets events, I must begin by trusting in the truth of its initial message. I can only hear and respond to its call if I have faith in the promise it makes: to speak in a language that will connect me with millions of unseen others who share the same tongue regardless of the content it conveys.

The conjuring of the nation as a virtual society mediated by a particular vernacular language, and transmitted by the invisible universality of telecommunication technologies, seems all too commonplace these days.[1] Still, its ability to fascinate and enthrall viewers who hear themselves addressed makes this phenomenon akin to a religious experience. It is useful here to recall the complex etymology of "religion," which comes from the Latin "religio" meaning obligation or bond. The root of "religio," however, is ambiguous. It comes both from "relegare" — formed by the prefix "re-" plus "legare," to gather, to harvest — and "religare," "re-" plus "ligare," to tie, and by extension to become indebted. These two senses of the word religion, at least in its Latin-Christian context, are both arguably integral to the Western understanding of the term.

On the one hand, "religion" refers to the experience of gathering in order to worship the sacred, which by definition is the unknowable and the infinite. On the other hand, it refers to taking on a debt, an obligation, and thus being held liable to the laws of calculation, exchange, and reciprocity prescribed by social conventions, and subject to ongoing negotiations. We can gloss this further to emphasize that religion posits a paradox. It is productive of social life, that is, a realm of secular and profane concerns — of publicity, rationality, and calculation — which realm is at the same time founded on something beyond and before sociality: on mystery, infinity, and the incalculable.

This sense of a before and a beyond that animate social life is what we might think of as religiosity. That sense exists prior to and in excess of institutionalized religion. I want to suggest that such religiosity is also an essential feature of national belonging, before and after the people are colonized by the state. Religiosity, like nation-ness, relates to the promise of going beyond one's present conditions, of becoming other than oneself, and of being taken up and transformed by something far greater than that self. To receive that promise is to suffer — in all senses of that term — the processes which bring it about.

We can give to these processes the name mediation (which of course is another term for conversion). Neither wholly transcendent nor wholly immanent, mediation is the state of in-between-ness which allows both for the emergence and overcoming of religious institutions that engage communities of believers (as well as non-believers). Religiosity as the experience of mediation thus entails dwelling in between dogmatism and ritual. It is a moment of secrecy at the limits of knowledge and at the threshold of faith. The religiosity inherent in national belonging does not come merely from submitting to the laws of the state, or the conventions of society, however unavoidable and necessary these may be. It also comes chiefly from the sense of momentary escape and freedom from their institutional and juridical constraints.

I propose that one way of understanding religion, society, and the state in the Philippines is to think through the historical tension between the existential nature of religiosity and the institutions of religion — between the open-endedness of mediation characteristic of religious experience, and the categorical hegemony typical of socio-cultural, religious, and political institutions. This is a task that is far more complicated and daunting than I can possibly do within the limits of this essay. In the interest of brevity, let me point to two powerful examples from the recent past.

Two of the most significant events that mark the last two decades of Filipino history are undoubtedly EDSA I and EDSA II, the civilian-led coups that ousted, respectively, Ferdinand and Imelda Marcos in 1986 and Joseph "Erap" Estrada in 2001. In most accounts, both events are regarded as more than the calculable and predictable outcomes of social movements and military discontent clashing with and overcoming massive corruption, economic decay, and state repression. They also speak about these events in religious terms as "miracles," the result of some sort of divine intervention that in part explains their non-violent means and morally satisfying ends. In both cases, the aftermath of the "miraculous" coup was marked by disappointment verging on despair, bitterness and cynicism, which stem from a deep sense of betrayal, of promises left unfulfilled, and of possibilities foreclosed. The experience of release from institutionalized oppression was followed by the return of the old order, though now sporting new acronyms and some new faces along with familiar ones. Similarly, the acute anticipation of justice so palpable in the two EDSAs was met by the recurrence if not intensification of the same old injustices, and a host of new ones as well. If God had momentarily intervened in human history, He also seems to have quickly fled, abandoning His people to their former captivity.

A key feature of both EDSAs was the use of telecommunication technologies for publicizing grievances and demands, announcing mass actions, and holding those in power accountable to international audiences. Analog media such as print, fax machines, the all important radio, and later television, were used in EDSA I, while digital media such as cell phones were deemed crucial in EDSA II.[2] The telecommunicative capacity of such media, whether analog or digital, was such that they permitted their users to send and receive messages from afar. Such messages consisted of a promiscuous mix of fact and fantasy, of threatening news and endless jokes, of rumors about the meaning of events and rumors about these rumors. The mixing of messages was generated by and generative of the mixing of social groups. Crowds made up of different classes and generations appeared on the streets, called by and calling upon whatever media was at their disposal. Gathering in the streets, they found themselves transformed, momentarily lifted from their individual identities and drawn to identify with a gathering whose limits were radically in flux. Caught in the renewed virtuality of a nation now set free from the state, they were plunged into a state of uncertainty, unable to predict, much less control, the unfolding of events.

In this context an important response emerged, especially during EDSA I but no less prominent in EDSA II: the widespread turn to prayer. The Latin-Christian underpinnings of lowland Philippine political culture, so adeptly delineated by historians such as John Schumacher and Reynaldo Ileto, undoubtedly account for the use of prayer as a way of dealing with the menacing uncertainty of these events.[3] As a kind of telecommunicative medium, prayer allows one to send and receive message from afar. Unlike print, radio, television, satellites, and cell phones, however, prayer prescribes the proper forms of speech and an indisputable destination of address: God.

One who prays seeks to reach what is beyond reach, and thereby sits in expectation of a miracle. Thus when miracles do happen, that is, when one receives an answer that one had hoped for, it will no longer be a surprise. Instead it will be something ready to have happened. "Miracles" in this sense are ratification of prayers. As supplications to change impending futures, prayers are fulfilled. Seen from the perspective of prayer, miraculous occurrences are not therefore miraculous at all. They are the returns resulting from an earlier investment. They are the materialization of proof and the realization of symbolic profit that reinforce one's faith.

The religious reading of the two EDSAs as "miracles" thus has a double aspect. On the one hand, it reaffirms the religiosity of EDSA as the moment when people found themselves unexpectedly beside themselves, swept by the processes of mediation, suspended between what I referred to earlier as the limits of knowledge and the threshold of faith. On the other hand, it domesticates each historical moment, shutting down the opening of an infinite eventfulness through the calculations of prayer. Both events contained the popular witnessing of the promise of justice in a future poised to arrive; yet in both events, many also shuddered at the terrifying prospects of what this future might hold. Such a future of violent upheaval was momentarily glimpsed during the reactionary "EDSA III," or what was dubbed in the newspapers as "poor people's power," launched by the followers of Estrada shortly after his ouster and hastily put down by the forces of the state.

The turn to prayer at EDSA I and II sought to restore a familiar order by way of calculated modes of address. The non-violence that marked both events similarly could be understood in at least two different but related ways. On the one hand, non-violence was about the patience and forbearance displayed by the crowd, their willingness to welcome the uncertainty of events and their readiness to forgive those who did not even ask for forgiveness. In this sense, non-violence involved the unconditional and radical hospitality of a people to that which is yet to come, and which has not even announced its coming. On the other hand, non-violence may also be understood as the result of fear that comes with the prospect of reckoning with past injustice and the prospect of revenge. Indeed, there were calls for vengeance on the part of those members of the masses who rallied for Estrada in the aftermath of EDSA II. The fear of taking on en masse the task of judgment and decision raises the specter of incalculable effects. Hearing the calls for retribution, rather than mere redistribution, from lumpen proletarians who on their part seemed to claim a kind of apocalyptic power to mete out justice, the middle class at EDSA II were no doubt afraid of the potential spiraling for violence.

"On the one hand and on the other hand": such was the ambivalence experienced at each of the first two EDSAs — the sense of being caught in between states, swept by the forces of transformation and mediation beyond individual and collective intentions. This is the experience of radical indecision, which is arguably the condition of possibility for arriving at any decision tout court. At once exhilarating and terrifying, this fundamental ambivalence has served as the touchstone of Filipino religiosity and the nation's modernity.

Something like it, I suspect, has marked the uncanny experience of nation-ness itself in many, perhaps all other, parts of the world in similar decisive moments. In the case of the Philippines, there is a sense of national pride associated with the events of 1986 and 2001 that led to the assertion of the people's collective power over that of the state. At the same time, there is an abiding fear, especially among the elites and the middle class, of what still another EDSA might bring. Occurring in excess of the legal and social limits of the dominant political culture, the religiosity evinced by these uprisings surpassed even the institutional hierarchy of the Catholic Church itself. Such uprisings tapped into the wellspring of revolutionary aspirations, which have deep roots in the nation's anti-colonial struggles, and which also challenged the social privileges and political power of elites. Hence, the prospect of future EDSAs generates the promise of redemption in a future yet to be announced, even as it raises the specter of a social revolution and the violent reckoning it would undoubtedly bring.

We can think of Filipino religiosity, then, as that which conveys the secret force of a history soaked in blood and steeped in death. It brings to mind not only the stirring calls for freedom, but also the ghostly voices calling for justice, which date back to the great revolution of 1896. Small wonder that the main beneficiaries of EDSA I and II, those who dominate Philippine society and politics today, find themselves in a bind. For they are both the inheritors and the targets of such ghostly calls, embodying while seeking to exorcise the spectrality of a nation colonized by the state.[4]

Fig. 19

Cardinal Sin for Free Election.
President Ferdinand Marcos, in power for twenty years, faced rising unrest after the assassination of his major opponent, Ninoy Aquino. When he called for a "snap election" to return himself to office and renew his public mandate, his critics strove for a genuine balloting. Here Jaime Cardinal Sin, after mass on 28 January 1986, reads a letter from the Catholic Bishops Conference of the Philippines on the subject, giving it the powerful imprimatur of his personal and symbolic support. (Tom Gralish, Philadelphia *Inquirer*)

Fig. 20

Volunteers Guarding Ballot Boxes. Canvassing of returns from Pasay City, among other places, was suspiciously slow. Here volunteers for the National Movement for a Free Election, one of them a nun, protect ballots against manipulation, 9 February 1986. (Tom Gralish, Philadelphia *Inquirer*)

Fig. 21

Corazon Aquino at Mass in Manila. Ninoy Aquino's widow, the opposition candidate, is given the freedom of the pulpit, 9 February 1986, to entreat her followers to keep faith during the counting of ballots. Her thumb and forefinger are extended in the symbolic gesture of her party, "L" for Laban. (Tom Gralish, Philadelphia *Inquirer*)

Fig. 22

Nuns Escort Soldiers Leaving Marcos Camp. A key event in the national crisis was the defections of the then vice-chief of staff of the armed forces, Gen. Fidel Ramos, and the Minister of Defense, Juan Ponce Enrile, to the Aquino side. Troops of like persuasion sought to leave Camp Aguinaldo, site of Marcos loyalists, for the dangerous walkable option of Camp Crame, headquarters of Gen. Ramos. Here, on 23 February 1986, nuns pray as they escort soldiers changing sides. (Tom Gralish, Philadelphia *Inquirer*)

Fig. 23

Ramos Hails Crowd as Marcos Flees. With news of Marcos flying to Hawaii in exile, Gen. Ramos assures an exuberant crowd in Camp Crame that the Aquino voters and followers are now, 24 February, in charge. Ramos, a Protestant, kept with him on public display during the crisis a statue of Our Lady of Fatima from his office. Here it is visible behind him. (Tom Gralish, Philadelphia *Inquirer*)

NOTES

[1] The notion of a virtual — or as it is more widely known, "imagined" — community to describe the nation is of course indebted to Benedict Anderson's classic work, *Imagined Communities: Reflections on the Origins and Spread of Nationalism* (London: Verso, 2nd edition, 1991). See also Anderson's *The Spectre of Comparisons: Nationalism, Southeast Asia and the World* (London: Verso, 1998). Two recent collections of essays on Anderson's work are also helpful in teasing out the broader implications of his arguments: Jonathan Culler and Pheng Cheah, eds., *Grounds of Comparison: Around the Work of Benedict Anderson* (New York: Routledge, 2003); and James T. Siegel and Audrey Kahin, eds., *Southeast Asia Over Three Generations: Essays Presented to Benedict O'G. Anderson* (Ithaca, NY: Cornell Southeast Asia Publications, 2003).

On the relationship between publicity, media, and the public sphere, the work of Jurgen Habermas, *The Structural Transformation of the Public Sphere: An Inquiry into a Category of Bourgeois Society*, trans. by Thomas Burger (Cambridge, MA: MIT Press, 1991), remains an indispensable point of reference. For tracing the links among telecommunication media, religion, and politics, I have been influenced by the works of Jacques Derrida, such as "Faith and Knowledge: The Two Sources of Religion at the Limits of Reason Alone," trans. by Samuel Weber in Gil Andajar, ed., *Acts of Religion* (New York: Routledge, 2002), pp. 40-100.

[2] For a discussion of digital media, especially cell phones in EDSA II, see Vicente L. Rafael, "The Cell Phone and the Crowd," *Public Culture*, 15, 3 (Fall 2003), pp. 399-425.

[3] For example, see John Schumacher, SJ, *Revolutionary Clergy: The Filipino Clergy and the Nationalist Movement, 1850-1903* (Quezon City: Ateneo de Manila University Press, 1981); and Reynaldo Ileto's highly influential book, *Pasyon and Revolution: Popular Movements in the Philippines, 1840-1910* (Quezon City: Ateneo de Manila University, 1979). For an earlier period, see Vicente L. Rafael, *Contracting Colonialism: Translation and Christian Conversion in Tagalog Society Under Early Spanish Rule* (Durham, NC: Duke University Press, 1993); while for the contemporary period, see Fenella Cannell's immensely insightful ethnography of folk Catholicism in Bicol province, *Power and Intimacy in the Christian Philippines* (Cambridge: Cambridge University Press, 1999).

[4] It is this historical conundrum, of the nation colonized by the state, that the hyphen in "nation-state" at once evokes and obscures; and which the history of the EDSAs recall again and again.

6

Reflections on Religion and Politics in the Philippines and Indonesia

Joel Rocamora

Religion and Social Identity

R eligion gets blamed for too much, yet not enough. Like other constructs of social meaning, religion is mobilized to serve the ends of the powerful, often leaving death and destruction in its wake.

From outside the region, some perceive Southeast Asia as the "second front" in the "fight against terrorism." After Afghanistan, before Iraq, President George W. Bush needed another front in his anti-terrorist war. Since the US invaded Iraq, however, Southeast Asia has receded into the background.

What nevertheless keeps Southeast Asia in the target sights of Bush's administration is anti-

Muslim prejudice in the West, especially the United States. Because there are more Muslims in Southeast Asia than in the Middle East, Americans assume that the region must be a hotbed of terrorist activity. There have been enough bombings — the horror of Bali on 10-12-02, two much smaller instances in Jakarta, and a smaller return to Bali — to make the claim seemingly plausible. In fact, Islamic fundamentalism and its militarized variants have limited influence in the region. Ordinary Islamic groups tend to be caught up in religious syncretism like everyone else there.

Since I am not a theologian, I might be forgiven for saying that "syncretism" is another way of saying "everyday life." With limited exceptions, in specific places and occasions, Southeast Asians tend to be more relaxed about religion than, say, South Asians or Arabs. As a result, religion gets played out in relation to other more dominant interests and identities. I am not saying that religion is not an important source of social and political identification in both the Philippines and Indonesia. On the contrary, it is vital in both countries. Islamic identity in particular is often expressed as resentment at not playing as big a role as its adherents think it should. This is true both in Indonesia, where Muslims constitute an overwhelming majority, and in the Philippines, where it is an overwhelmed minority.

Religion and Recent Politics

The resulting complexity is illustrated in the way religion is affecting politics in the two countries. In Indonesia, the electoral fortunes of Islamic political parties declined even further in the legislative and presidential elections in 2004. But the success of one relatively new Islamic party, PKS, shows that it is not the electoral drawing power of Islam that has declined, but the way that older parties have drawn on Islamic identity that is losing its appeal. The PKS is, if anything, more self-consciously Islamic than older Islamic parties. Instead of relaxed syncretist social and religious practices, the PKS asks its members to adhere to Islamic practice more strictly. In addition, it has also built a reputation as a "clean" party, and a fighter against corruption. Islamic parties, in other words, are accountable to standards that secular parties should also live by. In this, for all parties, PKS is presently, at least, a standard-bearer. And it carries its Islamic flag proudly.

The current crisis in the Philippines is an even better example of the complexity of the nexus between religion and politics. On July 8, 2005, within hours of each other, six cabinet secretaries and four other top government officials, the Liberal Party, a member of the administration coalition, former President Cory Aquino, a large group of civil society organizations, and the Association of Major Religious Superiors of the Philippines called for President Gloria Macapagal Arroyo to resign. The night before, the only remaining Filipino cardinal and two other bishops accompanied former President Aquino to the presidential palace to convey the same message. Two days later, however, the Catholic Bishops Conference of the Philippines (CBCP) came out with a statement that, in not calling on President Arroyo to resign, was widely interpreted as having prevented the downfall of the government.

How has the Catholic Church become such a crucial arbiter of political events, pro and con, in the Philippines? If we start only with recent history, the answer is fairly simple: the late Cardinal Jaime Sin. When Presidents Ferdinand Marcos (1986) and Joseph Estrada (2001) were overthrown in "People Power" mass actions, the people were called out to the streets by Cardinal Sin. After long illness, Cardinal Sin died in June 2005, very early in the present crisis. Without a highly political prelate to replace him, the members of the CBCP became vulnerable to what has been reported as a scolding from the new Pope delivered in no uncertain terms by the Papal Nuncio. The Nuncio reportedly said the Vatican is displeased over too much political interference by the local church and would no longer tolerate it. The bishops meekly obeyed.

Without an imprimatur from the official church, even the most vocal church leaders have been silenced. Key sections of the middle class who look to the church for guidance have so far refused to join the mounting calls for President Arroyo to resign. But even those who have called on the church to activism are ambivalent. As activist scholar Walden Bello puts it: "We cannot have it both ways. Bringing in the Church to help determine the resolution of a political crisis, even if desired resolution may be positive, will help legitimize its really negative role in obstructing progressive legislation and management in the area of reproductive and gender rights by the secular authorities."

Religion and Violence

Religion has played enough of a nasty role in various incidents of violence to give it a bad name. I am less concerned about *Jemaah Islamiya* — even less the *Abu Sayyaf* in the Philippines — than about violently militarized relationships between governments and rebel minorities. The *Abu Sayyaf* is a bandit group using religion as cover. They are both small groups operating in religious milieus not supportive of their murderous radicalism. The killings in Kalimantan, Sulawesi, and East Java in the last few years bother me more because I don't understand them. I don't believe religion alone is the substantive cause of those killings. Similar orgies of murder and mayhem, such as the killings of leftists in 1965-1966, took far more than religious inspiration — although Muslims confronting "atheistic communism" were a major factor.

If my main point — that religion in Philippine and Indonesian politics gets played out in relation to other, more powerful forces — is accurate, we then need to look carefully at those relationships. In Indonesia, secular political forces — Sukarno, Suharto, the military, the bureaucracy — have stood in the way of more effective translation of the Islamic majority in politics. Ironically, the fact that Muslims are a majority has meant that, more often than not, political contestation occurs chiefly among Muslim parties, rather than between them and secular parties such as the PDI-P and GOLKAR. The struggle in Aceh is often portrayed as an Islamic struggle. But it is, more than anything else, a struggle for control over lucrative natural resources. Apart from oil and natural gas, reports from there say that gangs controlling marijuana-growing cut across military and rebel ranks.

Understanding the tormented situation in the Philippine South requires going much further back in time. What is now the Philippines represented the outer edge of the expansion of Islam at the time the Spanish arrived in the 16th century. Muslim sultanates retained enough dynamism to successfully contest Spanish colonialism. Only the Americans succeeded in subjugating Muslim areas in Mindanao and Sulu. But Moro resistance exacted tremendous social costs. Moro society was mobilized for warfare for several centuries with attendant stagnation of political institutions. The migration of Christian settlers in the second half of the last century pushed Moros into economic penury in a smaller and smaller part of their old homeland.

Christian chauvinism of Spanish and American colonizers, later Filipino central government authorities, took many different forms. One of the most pernicious, because most easily justified as well-meaning "integration," was the cooptation of Moro leaders. What was involved here was not religious conversion, but the attenuation of Moro categories of social and political meaning. Moro leaders in Manila not only had to dress different, they also had to learn to talk and think different. Since back home they had to revert to Moro culture, one can only imagine their state of political and intellectual exhaustion. Since their place in Manila politics was assured through their diluted "Moro-ness," they had even less incentive to represent constituent interests than Christian local politicians.

The icons of Moro resistance in the past century were traditional leaders like Kamlon who simply opted out — refused to live under the "laws" of the government and became "outlaws." The first modern Moro movement, the Moro National Liberation Front (MNLF), was modern mainly in the sense that it mobilized Moro armed resistance in service to the assertion of a Bangsa Moro as a political entity, which precluded piecemeal cooptation of Moro leaders. It was led by university-educated youth, most of whom were not from the Moro aristocracy. This leadership was not religious, but it was able to recruit a base only by asserting "Moro-ness" — a social category made religious only by Christian chauvinism.

The MNLF was significant because it succeeded in becoming a social movement — in projecting a new category of political meaning and action for Moros. Unfortunately, after many years of struggle, in 1996 the MNLF leadership agreed to a political settlement with the central government which, more than anything else, meant a return to old-style Manila government cooptation of individual Moro leaders. Indeed, many senior MNLF leaders subsequently got elected to local government positions with the support of then President Fidel Ramos. When MNLF leader Nur Misuari realized that the central government would not deliver what it promised, and he attempted to return to tactical armed threats, a large group of his former lieutenants, all of whom now occupied cushy government positions, opposed him.

The Moro Islamic Liberation Front (MILF) split from the MNLF more than a decade ago. It is still fighting the government on and off. It provides an interesting contrast to the MNLF in a number of ways. Apart from the fact that its social base is different from that of the MNLF, it also has a more distinctly Islamic character. Its leadership comes from a corps of ulama trained at the al-Azhar University in Cairo over a period of years. Apart from funding scholarships, Libya and Saudi Arabia also funded the construction of mosques and the operation of madrasahs. In the process, the traditional practice of Islam has been renewed in Mindanao-Sulu.

Hashim Salamat, the late leader of the MILF, was one of these students. The Council of Ulama in the MILF is a powerful leadership body. On first inspection, it appears to me that Islam has provided the "ideological" basis for the greater staying power of the MILF. The same might be said of the GAM in Aceh. The fact that both movements appear to be close to concluding peace agreements with their central governments is one of the more encouraging recent developments in the region. If we presume a positive value to the maintenance of the Moro and Acehnese social movements, it would follow that religion has played an important, progressive role in these instances. But how do we convince the Manila and Jakarta governments of this? Is anti-Muslim chauvinism the only obstacle? Or is the very way we conceive of church and state relations too limited to encompass the varieties of political expressions of religion?

Separation, Solidarity, Democracy

Western conceptions of state and religion calling for their separation springs from the logic of the Great Inquisition. Although I come from the one country in the region most deeply affected by Roman Catholic inquisitions great and small, I will not claim Asian exceptionalism. The use of religion by the powerful everywhere, Asia included, provides an argument for separation wherever religion continues to assert social power. In Western Europe, the home of conceptions of separation of church and state, empty churches now obviate the strict need for separation. In Asia, however, mosques and churches are full. Do we need here to assert the same wall between church and state?

The powerful use religion one way; the poor, another. Centuries of peasant rebellions in the Philippines were fueled by the broken promises of Roman Catholicism and by the assertion of its millenarian promise of deliverance. Although the Communist Party of the Philippines will not acknowledge it, the anti-dictatorship struggle fed off of the same millenarian tradition, albeit renamed as theology of liberation. Political reformers in Indonesia want to get rid of primordial loyalties represented, among others, by the Nahdatul Ulama and Muhammadiyah. Do they want in its place the unalloyed personalism of Philippine politics?

If we cannot — should not — remove constitutional strictures separating church and state, and at the same time cannot prohibit various dimensions of religious solidarity which, willy-nilly, will find their ways to politics, what can we do? To start with, we can work to remove the political obstacles to the assertion of other solidarities in politics, most importantly those of class and other oppressions. Then we need to admit that secular sectarianism prevents many of us from seeing how important religion can be to the struggles of the poor. Finally, we need to recognize that democracy is not neat, easy, or logical, precisely because it has to be negotiated.

Fig. 24

Magsaysay Visited by Muslim Women. In the years of his presidency before
death in an air crash (1953-1957), Magsaysay made clear his sympathy with the
oppressed and his accessibility to minorities. In 1956 a deputation from the
Moslem Women's Association of the Philippines, led by Princess Tarhata and
Mrs. Pintoy, meets with him in his office. Earlier, Mrs. Magsaysay had consented
to be their honorary advisor. (Ramon Magsaysay Award Foundation)

Fig. 25

Protestant Church Ablaze in Mataram. As part of the semi-anarchy of that
time, Christians and Muslims fought in parts of eastern Indonesia. Following a
mass meeting, 17 January 2000, Muslim youth burn down a church. (Supriyanto
Khafid, TEMPO)

Fig. 26

Luis Taruc and Nur Misuari, 14 February 2004. Luis Taruc, former leader of the Hukbalahap rebels, spent sixteen years in jail. Here he visits Nur Misuari, former leader of the Moro National Liberation Front, in military detention. [Dik Trofeo, collection of the editor] Peasant or socioeconomic consciousness rarely intersects with ethnoreligious consciousness in the Philippines. But here Taruc persuades Misuari to cosign with him a "Valentine Day Covenant of Love." The two pledged "minds, hearts, and soul…humbly beseeching Allah/God to bless… the Future of Dear Motherland." Exactly one year later, on Valentine's Day 2005, Islamic militants of a different mindset engineered three time-coordinated bomb blasts across the Philippines, in Manila, Cotobato, and Davao.

Fig. 27

Huk Veterans Meet at Church. In San Luis, Pampanga, hometown of Luis Taruc, an 18th century church is a gathering point for veterans of a rebellion quelled over half a century before. Slightly earlier, 2,500 had assembled. Taruc [here, in brown cap, with right hand on walker] died in April 2005, less than a year after this reunion. [Dik Trofeo, collection of the editor]

7

One Nation Under God? History, Faith, and Identity in Indonesia

Donald K. Emmerson

O ne nation, one people, one language, *one religion*?

Definitely not. The nationalist authors of the Youth Oath of 1928 left religion off their list of things they simultaneously claimed "Indonesia" was, hoped it would be, and pledged to see it become — one country with a single people united by the same Indonesian language.

In 1928 the only plausible candidate for a national religion was Islam. Its adherents formed a vast majority in the Netherlands Indies. They do so today in the colony's successor — the Republic of Indonesia. According to census data, Muslim predominance stood at 87.5 percent in 1971 and 88.2 percent in 2000, while Christians in those years, respectively, were pegged at 7.4 and 8.9 percent of the population, with even smaller percentages assigned to Hindus (1.9 and 1.8), Buddhists (0.9 and 0.8), and "Others" (1.4 and 0.2).[1]

Indonesian Islam underwent a resurgence in the late 20th century. Striking in this light is a rarely noted anomaly: From 1971 to 2000, while both Christians and Muslims gained shares, Christians did so more rapidly than Muslims. The census figures are estimates; their precision is misleading. They do nevertheless suggest that Islamization was inward not outward — a gain in quality more than quantity — and that Indonesian Christians, for all the vicissitudes they have experienced, are hardly a vanishing group. Leo Suryadinata and his colleagues, on whose invaluable presentation of these data I rely, believe that in 1971-2000, while the Muslim population was expanding at an average 1.86 percent per year — a rate indistinguishable from the 1.83 annual growth of the Indonesian population as a whole — Indonesian Christians grew 2.48 percent per year.[2]

These statistics are essential to understanding why, in 1928, for Indonesian Islamists, upholding a vast-majority faith and installing that faith as a pillar of national identity were such different things. Religion — Islam — was not included among the unities so hopefully announced in the Youth Oath because it was uniquely divisive: *normatively exclusive, internally diverse,* and, especially to the non-Muslim minority, *numerically threatening.*

Calling for the Islamization of Indonesia would have forced upon non-Muslims an ugly choice: convert, suffer, or leave. Compared with choosing a religion, speaking a language was far less problematic. Belonging to an ethnic group with its own mother tongue did not preclude being and speaking Indonesian. But you could not be a mainstream Muslim and consider yourself a Catholic, a Protestant, a Hindu, or a Buddhist at the same time. Islamist hostility to apostasy made it difficult to do so even at different points in time: Once a Muslim, always so. Orthodox Islam was and remains *normatively exclusive.*

That a normatively exclusive religion could be *internally diverse* only seems paradoxical. Among self-defined Muslims, realities differed from the norm. The main stream was not the sole stream. Most notably, over much of the 20th century, "Javanese religion" asserted and accommodated heterodoxy inside Islam, syncretic borrowings included. But already in 1912 in the central Javanese city of Yogyakarta a mosque official, K. H. Ahmad Dahlan, led the forging of a modernist Muslim organization Muhammadiyah, or Followers of the Prophet Muhammad, precisely to scrape accreted Javanist barnacles off the ship of faith. In 1926, just two years before the Youth Oath was declared, the controversy intensified with the counter-founding of Nahdlatul Ulama — a rurally based Revival of Religious Scholars unwilling to be sidelined by Muhammadiyah's modernist recourse directly to the Qur'an and Hadith.

Because of this diversity, Islam in Indonesia has resisted reification into a hermetic or even a consistent whole. Reflecting but also reinforcing this multistrandedness was Clifford Geertz's influential 1960 trisection of *The Religion of Java* into three variants — orthodox *santri*, yes, but also *abangan* and *priyayi*.[3] In contrast to the seeming homogeneity of Arabized Islam in the Middle East, the Javanese variety became noted for its variegation — decentered, open, theologically laissez faire. Nor was this understanding to be found among Indonesianists alone. Long focused on the Middle East, Bernard Lewis visited Java briefly in 1989 to lecture on Islam to Muslim audiences. Afterwards he remarked: "They were so relaxed!"[4]

Cross-regional impressions aside, few would deny that the salience and character of Indonesian Islam have changed over time, since 1928. A full historical account would chart the waxing and waning of Islamism since precolonial times. Such a narrative would end with an upswing in Islamist imagery, orthodoxy, and militancy dating from the late decades of the 20th century.[5]

If green is the color of Islam, Indonesia's demography has been verdant. As already noted, "Muslim" is what nearly nine-tenths of Indonesians have told census-takers they are. But those nine-tenths have never formed a monolithic bloc. Aside from the country's non-Muslims, heterodox Muslims, liberal Muslims, secular Muslims, and merely non- or semi-practicing or otherwise "relaxed" Muslims have also had reason to wonder just how light or deep or dappled their archipelago's variously Islamic greenery was going to be. As the pattern fluctuated over time between *Islam statistiek* and *Islam fanatiek* — between being, respectively, "Muslim" only in name or "Muslim" in militant word and deed — the sheer bulk of this vast majority appeared more or less *numerically threatening* to Indonesians anxious lest their body politic turn deeply green enough to grow an intolerantly "Islamic" state.

On a national scale, it never happened. Islamists hoping to translate the numerical predominance of Muslims into a fully Islamized society under an Islamic state repeatedly failed to achieve their aims. In effect, history thwarted demography. More precisely, the moderation of mainstream Muslims and the fears of non-Muslims combined to foil those few hard-line Islamists who wanted the state to impose Islamic law on all Indonesian Muslims. In 2004 the memory of this prolonged and ongoing failure still rankled in the minds of the defeated fringe.[6] And some of the many Indonesians who feared that fringe's radical agenda were less than fully reassured by its failure. In their anxious eyes, the largest national Muslim society anywhere retained its potential someday to sustain a theocracy — and thereby implement demography's eventual revenge.

Just how history trumped demography lies beyond my allotted space. A longer essay could explain Islamism's ups and downs in tandem with changes in society, politics, economics, and technology. Above such facts on the ground, however, in the last half of the 20th century, there were phrases in the air. Notably enduring and contending among these bits of script were seven words and five principles launched in the republic's founding year, 1945 — language directly relevant to the question whether Indonesia could ever become "one nation under Allah."

The seven words[7] would have empowered the state to enforce Islamic laws for all Muslims. Had Islamist politicians succeeded in their decades-long effort to include this injunction in the Indonesian constitution, the state would have been tasked, in effect, to render a patchwork-pastel Muslim majority more deeply and thoroughly green. In 1945, in the first of a series of defeats for the amendment's supporters, the drafters of Indonesia's first constitution failed to include the seven words. The amendment, Sukarno argued, would have split the country as it was being born. The makers of Indonesia's first national charter chose instead to adorn that document with Sukarno's paradigmatically nationalist Five Principles, or Pancasila. One of these principles did, however, accommodate the stress on monotheism that is typical of political Islam by including in the new state's philosophy "Belief in a Supremely Singular God."[8]

If this injunction was ambiguous then, it remains elastic now. Depending on how it is spun, it can be rendered *negligible, eclectic, selected,* or *Islamist.*

Negligible: It is reasonable to think that in the daily lives of ordinary Indonesians, Pancasila does not matter much. Ideological debates among elites need not always trigger contending interpretations in society at large. Absent ongoing controversy as to what the monotheistic precept in Pancasila "really" means, it may be solemnly invoked at independence-day celebrations every 17 August and pretty much forgotten for the rest of the year. In a future Indonesia where national identity based on pluralist tolerance has been institutionalized to the point of being taken entirely for granted — a rosy scenario — citizens may not take Pancasila seriously because they no longer need to.

Eclectic: An alternative to treating the religious credo in Pancasila as negligibly symbolic is to assign it the widest possible scope. If the fullest tolerance — the biggest tent — is desired, "Belief in a Supremely Singular God" can be made to label and shelter almost any creed, including mystical appreciations of the unity of the universe and the argument that all religions are alike and equivalent in praising and sharing the same single deity. On this interpretive map, all religious roads, as it were, lead to Rome. When he floated Pancasila, back in 1945, Sukarno was eclectic in this unitarian sense.[9]

Selected: Equating religions is blasphemous to Islamists. For these believers, only Islam is complete and true, and the Christian Trinity smacks of polytheism. Without narrowing monotheism to faith in Allah alone, the state can name the specific religions that it deems to revere a "Supremely Singular God." The result is a selection of faiths that have been officially certified as monotheistic, however arbitrary such labeling may be.

Selection summarizes Indonesian experience. Already, in August 1945, just two months after the enunciation of Pancasila by Sukarno, he and other nationalists had appeased Islamist feeling by promoting monotheism from fifth to first place and writing a revised version of the series into the preamble of Indonesia's first constitution. There the pentad was made the basis of the new state. The 1945 constitution has remained continuously in effect since 1959. Recent amendments have not altered the preamble. But the monotheistic principle has not escaped reinterpretation.

Sukarno's successor as president, Suharto, fully in office from 1968 to 1998, limited the scope of the tenet to belief in one of a Big Five: Islam, Protestantism, Catholicism, Hinduism, or Buddhism — full stop.[10] Disallowed, by implication, were syncretism across religions and deviation from one-God orthodoxy within any of the permitted five faiths. While retaining its constitutional status as a leading element of state ideology, monotheism in this five-part sense became as well, in 1985, a legally required credo of Suharto's authoritarian regime.

How on earth (or in heaven) could anyone monotheize a faith so blatantly polytheistic as Hinduism, or one so atheistic as Buddhism? *Raison d'état*? Seeing like a state?[11] Perhaps so. But one can also see in this cut-to-fit metaphysics a modestly placating gesture toward the most supremely and self-consciously monolithic theism of the lot — orthodox Islam. And that thought segues into a third way of spinning the one-God *sila*.

Islamist: However preferable even an implausible accreditation of monotheisms may have been compared with wide-open eclecticism, the Big Five turnstiles through which state-defined "monotheists" could pass were still necessarily unacceptable to Indonesian Muslims committed to the idea that theirs was the sole true religion. Yet allegiance to Pancasila had become mandatory. What to do?

One could, of course, reject Suharto's dogma and risk the consequences. A few did. But other Islamists opted to do some theological engineering of their own, by Islamizing what had become the first *sila*. And this at least involved a lot less casuistry than did the state's decapitation of the Hindu hydra, or its recapitation of headless Buddhism. For Pancasila's first credo in Indonesian — *Ketuhanan yang Maha Esa* — could by changing a few letters be narrowed to an exclusively Islamic statement: *Ketauhidan yang Maha Esa*, meaning "Islamic Belief in Allah — the One and Only Supremely Singular God." The Big Five shorn of the little four would thus leave only the Big One: Islam.

In this respect, and in retrospect, for all the rhetoric of eclectic tolerance with which Sukarno first conveyed Pancasila in June 1945, its monotheism did open an opportunity for Islamist nationalists, in effect, to amend the 1928 Youth Oath by adding a controversial fourth basis for Indonesian identity: one nation, one people, one language, *one religion* — Islam. Islamists never dared to propose such an amendment and suffer the backlash that would have ensued. Yet the future possibility of interpreting *Ketuhanan* as *Ketauhidan* remains: Islamization not against Pancasila but by means of it.

Suharto's New Order is gone. Indonesians are freer to criticize Pancasila than they were under his regime. A hard-line Islamist today is more likely to deride and dismiss Pancasila than to bother appropriating it through wordplay. A case in point is Abu Bakar Ba'asyir, the radical who heads the Council of Indonesian Jihadists (Majelis Mujahiddin Indonesia) and has been identified as the spiritual eminence of the reportedly terrorist Islamic Congregation (Jemaah Islamiyah).

Ba'asyir and his few fellow jihadists are greatly outnumbered by mainstream political Muslims who are nonviolent and willing to work within the political system, including voting for parties with more or less Islamist identities and agendas. Generally speaking, in these larger and more moderate circles, Pancasila is not an infidel plot, nor even an unalterably rival design. Even a suspicious Islamist politician knows that the five principles were not wholly discredited by Suharto's unpopularity and downfall in 1998. Of the 24 parties competing in the national legislative election held on 4 April 2004, 15 were self-identified with Pancasila — triple the five that based themselves on Islam.[12]

If violence wielded against difference is the ultimate expression of intolerance, political Islamists are, by that measure, more tolerant than jihadists.[13] The chance of a militantly Islamist state coming to power by violence in Indonesia is nil. And while they outnumber jihadists, nonviolently political Islamists in Indonesia are a historically diminished minority. Despite Islam's nine-tenths majority, in the April 2004 voting for the national legislature, only 21 percent of all valid ballots went to one of the five Islam-based parties. The most successful of these was the Unity Development Party, or PPP, with only 8 percent of the vote, down from 11 percent in the legislative election of 1999. Clearly, most Indonesian Muslim voters do not support avowedly Muslim parties.[14]

Islamist support does appear to have increased in April 2004 compared with the legislative election of June 1999. The historical trend has been downward, however. Comparing the results of legislative voting in 2004 and 1955, it would appear that over a half-century, support for Islamist parties as a proportion of all votes fell roughly in half.[15]

There was little good news for Islamists in the results of Indonesia's first-ever direct presidential election on 5 July 2004. Of the five candidates for the top office, the one most exclusively associated with Islam was the PPP's Hamzah Haz, and he drew the fewest votes — just 3 percent. Another losing candidate with an Islamic background, Amien Rais, won 15 percent of the vote. But he presented himself and his party as open to all Indonesians. All ten of the candidates, including the five running for vice president, were Muslims. But none advocated an Islamic state. Nine of the ten refrained out of conviction; they did not want a theocratic future for Indonesia. As for Hamzah Haz, in an ideal world he might have welcomed Islamist rule, but he knew that the Islamic-state project had become a third rail in Indonesian politics.

In view of these conditions, it is tempting to preclude for the republic any Islamist future at all. But if the moderation that still marks most Indonesian Muslims continues to forestall either secularism or fanaticism, another possibility could arise. It could just conceivably be that sometime in this century, a distinctively Indonesian Islam — a moderate, tolerant, vast-majority Islam whose adherents will steadfastly refuse to use their suffrage to elect a divisively Islamic state — will take its place alongside the one nation, the one people, and the one language of 1928 as the one loosely defining religion of the republic.

This is a long-shot possibility. It is by no means a prediction. Nor can I predict the future repercussions of Islamist violence — including deadly jihadist bombings twice each in Bali and Jakarta since October 2002, and Muslim-Christian clashes in Maluku and Sulawesi intermittently since 1999. But the lesson that Indonesians appear to have drawn from these cases is not that jihad works, or that it ought to work, or that the country can afford to indulge or ignore major Islamist attacks. It is rather that the costs of such violence are too great to sustain — in fatalities, damage, impoverishment, national embarrassment, and foreign reprehension. For whatever combination of reasons, as of mid-2005 in Indonesia, democracy was not about to usher in an Islamic state.

The risk is not that Indonesian voters will warrant Islamist intolerance, but rather that nonviolent political Islamists may in future elections fail to do well enough in votes and seats to keep them all peaceably within the country's evolving democratic system.

Much will depend on the balance of overlap and tension between Islamism on the one hand and nationalism on the other — and on developments that Indonesians cannot control. Consider the extreme global downside: What if (and it's a huge if) Americans are in the early stages of a long and borderless struggle between fanatic partisans of an Islamist jihad and no-less-Manichean wagers of Judeo-Christian-secularist counter-jihad? Then one can imagine Indonesia reverting to a variation on its anti-colonial past.

Other things being equal, the more unanimously Indonesians abhor American policy, including its Zionist tilt, the greater the inducement for Islamists to become nationalist and for nationalists to become Islamist. If colonialism unified its Indonesian opponents in the last century, in this one a lethal conjoining of Americanism with Christianism, Zionism, secularism, liberalism, and unilateralism could foster a new and increasingly Islamist Indonesian nationalism. And this could flourish with or without turning the islands into grounds for an Islamic state.

Some analysts might reply, against this worst-case speculation, that the very idea of Islamist nationalism is oxymoronic, that Islam is resolutely transnational and antinational, that it aims not to reinforce but to dissolve the inter-state borders that now separate Muslim societies. But the millennial and world-girdling dream of a resurrected caliphate that inspires some Islamists is not prophylactic against either the nationalization of Islamism or the Islamization of nationalism. It may be instructive to recall in this context how a comparably global fantasy of Marxism — the eventual withering away of states — failed to keep Communism and nationalism neatly apart during the Cold War.

Nor is American nationalism safe from chiliastic Christianism. If Americans want to understand and respond to the present intersecting of religion and politics in the world, they would do well to pay attention not only to the history of Indonesia and other mainly Muslim societies. Relevant too are the connotations and controversies that have surrounded the bits of civic scripture posted by America's founding fathers, including the Cold War-driven self-identification of the United States as one nation, "under God."

In 2003-2004 an atheist challenged the phrase "under God" in the American pledge of allegiance.[16] This is not conceivable in Indonesia. But the controversy may usefully remind American observers of Indonesia that it is not just in "new nations" that questions of national identity are debated — and that it takes more than a high standard of living to settle them.[17]

As for the Bush administration, reportedly then-Senator and now-Attorney General John Ashcroft had this to say to an audience in 1999 at Bob Jones University, which had just awarded him an honorary degree:

> Unique among the nations, America recognized the source of our character as being Godly and eternal, not being civic and temporal. And because we have understood that our source is eternal, America has been different. *We have no king but Jesus.*[18]

An American Pancasila the Pledge of Allegiance is not. Yet the words "under God" are amenable to different American interpretations — *negligible, eclectic, selected,* or *Christianist* — already familiar to historians of Indonesia. And the American experience does at least bring to mind a future for religion and the state in Indonesia that is milder than the Armageddon intimated above.

What that alternative future entails, it seems to me, is the valorization of the belief, already widespread among Indonesian Muslims, that neither their piety, their identity, nor their self-confidence depends upon validation, let alone enforcement, by the state. That peaceable future may also involve, contrary to the solidarity with militantly Islamist Arabs that the ongoing Palestinian tragedy feeds in Indonesia, a rising aversion among the islands' Muslims to attempts to Arabize their religion. The virulence and violence of fiercely Islamist groups, whose leaders are disproportionally of Arab (e.g., Yemeni) descent, has already triggered criticism among more moderate and liberal Indonesian Muslims.[19]

To revisit the future one more time: Between terminal apocalypse and workable accommodation, the latter is far more likely. Yet majority-Muslim Indonesia will not become a nation that is only symbolically "under God" — civically, ceremonially, without sectarian controversy — except to the extent that Muslims themselves feel comfortable about their state and their religion, including respect for their religion by the state. Beyond theology and slogans hung in the air, much will depend on whether the country's nascent democracy can make concrete progress on a non-religious agenda — less crime, more jobs, less corruption, better health and education — and thereby help weaken credence in state-dictated Islamism as the sole escape from troubled times.

Barring an Indonesian Ataturk or Ayatollah, and assuming some kind of democracy survives: The more secure and less resentful Muslims become, the safer all Indonesians will be from intolerantly regimist[20] or state-fostered Islam. Ironically, this seemingly "secular" outcome could eventually prove a boon to faith — a private faith relaxed enough to render harmless the prospect, so fearsome in the 20th century, that Indonesia could become "one nation, one people, one language, one religion."

Although an Islamic state will remain hard to imagine and divisive to implement, that need not be true of an ethically "Islamic" but politically secular civil society — a *masyarakat madani* whose link to Medina is no more than etymological.[21] Then again, like other wishfully thinking observers of Indonesian Islam, I did not anticipate the scattered but deadly outbreaks of jihadist violence that have marred the country's transition from authoritarian rule. Once burned, twice shy.

The fact remains that in recent years Indonesians have experienced three democratic elections — legislative in June 1999 and again in April 2004, presidential in July-September 2004 — that affirmed how truly marginal to the country's political life extremist Muslims are.

Thrice heartened, once bold — or just bold enough to conclude that although the Youth Oath of 1928 will not be formally amended, one can conjecture with due caution along these lines:

If democracy and a correspondingly civic culture take hold; *if* Indonesians and their elected leaders make real headway in solving the country's many pressing problems; and *if* "Western" and "Muslim" civilizations do not in the meantime collide . . . then the idea of Indonesia as one nation under one vaguely Islamic but mainly inclusive and tolerant God could be conceivable after all.

Having begun with a question, however, I cannot resist ending with one. Is this benign prospect crippled by its ifs — or not? That I leave to readers to decide.

Fig. 28

Sukarno, the Voice of Pancasila. The President of the newly proclaimed Republic of Indonesia appears in a military uniform he devised for the revolutionary situation against the Dutch. (Library of Congress, LC-USZ62-105693) Earlier in that year, April 1945, in a hasty constitutional convention assembled under the Japanese Military Administration, Sukarno had delivered his great speech on Pancasila, the five organizing principles for the new nation. Despite hyper-dogmatic application under Suharto, especially from the late 1970s through the late 1980s, these principles remain essential to the fabric of Indonesian nationhood: belief in a Supreme Being, nationalism, democracy, social justice, and humanitarianism.

Fig. 29

Laskar Jihad. The largest of several hyper-Islamist volunteer forces prominent at the time (April 2000), the Laskar Jihad allegedly had 10,000 fighters at its high point. (Kemal Jufri, IMAJI) In warring against Christians in Maluku, Sulawesi, and Papua, they defined their opponents as "belligerent infidels," which gave them a religious justification for killing. Later, careful police investigation of the bombing in Bali (12 October 2002), which murdered over 200 foreign tourists and Indonesians, revealed undeniable connections with international terrorism. Laskar Jihad claimed to have rebuffed overtures from Al Qaeda. But in a new atmosphere of Indonesian public mistrust of militant Islam, it announced that it had disbanded.

Fig. 30

Abdurrahman Wahid as President. Under a chandelier in the Istana Merdeka, Gus Dur stands posed as the second successive distinctively Muslim president of democratic Indonesia. (Kemal Jufri, IMAJI) But the three years of Habibie, who took over from the deposed Suharto (May 1998), through the impeachment of Wahid (succeeded by the secular Megawati, July 2001), apparently demonstrated to most Indonesians that there was no magic in having a Muslim as president.

NOTES

[1] Leo Suryadinata, Evi Nurvidya Arifin, and Aris Ananta, *Indonesia's Population: Ethnicity and Religion in a Changing Political Landscape* (Singapore: Institute of Southeast Asian Studies, 2003), pp. 104-105.

[2] Suryadinata et al., *Indonesia's Population*, pp. 104-105.

[3] Clifford Geertz, *The Religion of Java* (Glencoe, IL: Free Press, 1960).

[4] Quoting from a conversation at his home in Princeton, NJ. Lewis may be considered the doyen of Islamologists writing in English.

[5] Along these lines, see M. C. Ricklefs, *A History of Modern Indonesia since c. 1200* (3rd ed., Houndmills, Basingstoke, UK: Palgrave, 2001).

[6] In mid-2004 a hard-line Islamist journal *Sabili* amply illustrated this resentment. One contributor, e.g., bemoaned the "collective amnesia" of (moderate) Muslims — an "acute sickness" that had prevented them from remembering how the Muslim community had been "shoved into the same hole, time and time again." It would take patience and a "clever knockout blow" against the enemies of Islam to get out of that hole once and for all

— that is, for the Muslim mass to climb up out of its inferior role as a merely "statistical majority" to become an effective "political majority" in Indonesia. (Kamarudin, "Pasar Politik Islam," *Sabili*, Special Issue: *Islam Kawan atau Lawan* (July 2004), p. 183 [of 182-184].)

[7] In Indonesian, the words are: "… *dengan kewajiban menjalankan syariat Islam bagi pemeluk-pemeluknya.*" "*Pemeluk-pemeluknya*" means "those who embrace it." If "it" refers to "*Islam*" as a religion, the phrase could mean "… with implementing Islamic law obligatory for Muslims," and that could indeed imply a mandate to the state to require all Muslims to observe Islamic laws whether they agree with them or not. A more plausible translation, however, would take *pemeluk-pemeluknya* to mean those who embrace Islamic law (*syariat Islam*). Can one embrace Islam without embracing Islamic law? The answer is yes in the minds of the many Indonesian Muslims for whom Islam is a personal, ethical, or mystical but not a legalistic faith. Would this translation of the seven words leave these anti-legalist Muslims free from punishment by official enforcers of Islamic law? Arguably, yes. The seven words never having been enacted since the constitution was first adopted, this benign understanding of their consequences has never arisen. In the unlikely future event of the words' inclusion in the constitution, one might see a burgeoning of anti-legalist — Sufi? — Islam among Muslims eager to escape their reach. The benign meaning would, in any event, outrage orthodox Muslims unable to countenance the separation of Islam from Islamic law. It is probably the fear of triggering such rage that has kept out of public discourse the grammatically more accurate interpretation of the seven words.

[8] A typical rendering of the Indonesian phrase into English is "Belief in One Supreme God," or words to that same effect. This amounts to treating, in the original Indonesian, *Ketuhanan yang Maha Esa*, the Sanskritic terms *Maha* and *Esa* as separate adjectives — in turn, "Supreme" and "One." But *Maha* could be understood by many Indonesians who encounter or recite the phrase as an adverb that intensifies *Esa*, making God "Supremely One" or "Supremely Singular." This phrasing is consistent with my understanding of the adverbial usage of *maha* in compound expressions such as *maha kuasa*, which I believe means not "supreme and powerful" but "omnipotent," or *maha besar*, which I take to convey not "supreme and big" but "huge."

[9] See "Pidato Bung Karno,"http://www.megaforpredisent.org/bk/bk_5_5.htm, p. 8.

[10] Though mainly eclectic, Sukarno was not consistently so. In 1965 he bowed to selectivity by according official recognition to a Big Six: the above-mentioned five plus Confucianism. Nor was Suharto, himself something of a Javanist, always selective. But in 1979 his cabinet decertified Confucianism, leaving the Big Five.

[11] Compare this innovatively Procrustean theology-by-fiat with the cases cited in James C. Scott, *Seeing like a State: How Certain Schemes to Improve the Human Condition Have Failed* (New Haven, CT: Yale University Press, 1998).

[12] Calculated from "Election 2004: The Old, the New and the Not So New — An Overview of the 24 Political Parties Competing in the 2004 General Elections," *Van Zorge Report on Indonesia*, 6: 2-3 (9 March 2004), pp. 5-25, where the remaining four parties are listed as committed to Nationalism-Socialism (2), Marhaenism (1), and Justice, Democracy, and Welfare (1).

[13] Within Islamic discourse, I mean by "jihadist" a person or persons advocating or engaged in violence in pursuit of what the Prophet Muhammad is said to have called the "lesser jihad" — *jihad asghar* — in contrast to the nonviolent tenor of the activities covered by what he is thought to have labeled the "greater jihad" — *jihad akbar*. Needless to add, even within the Muslim world, let alone without, jihad is an intensely contested concept.

[14] The 21 percent figure was calculated from official data in Komisi Pemilihan Umum (KPU), "Pemilu 2004: Hasil Perhitungan Suara: Rekapitulasi Perolehan Suara Sah untuk DPR-RI," http://www.kpu.go.id/suara/hasilsuara_dpr_sah. php, including the PPP's 8 percent. That party's 1999 figure is from Dwight King, *Half-hearted Reform: Electoral Institutions and the Struggle for Democracy in Indonesia* (Westport, CT: Praeger, 2003), p. 78 (Table 4.1).

[15] Compare, e.g., Saiful Mujani and R. William Liddle, "Indonesia's Approaching Elections: Politics, Islam, and Public Opinion," *Journal of Democracy*, 15: 1 (January 2004), p. 112 [full pp. 108-123]; or King, *Half-hearted Reform*, p. 126.

[16] Linda Greenhouse, "Atheist Presents Case for Taking God from Pledge" and "One Crucial Issue in Pledge Case: What Does 'Under God' Mean?" in *The New York Times*, 25 and 22 March 2004, respectively.

[17] A case in point is Samuel Huntington's *Who Are We? The Challenges to America's National Identity* (New York: Simon & Schuster, 2004) and the critical reviews it received, e.g., in the May-June 2004 *Foreign Affairs*.

[18] Was Ashcroft being nice to his host? Or was he being sincere? Likely both. My source for this quote is Farid Esack, "In Search of Progressive Islam beyond 9/11," in Omid Safi, ed., *Progressive Muslims: On Justice, Gender and Pluralism* (Oxford, UK: Oneworld, 2003), p. 96, n. 30 [full pp. 78-97]; italics mine.

[19] An illustration is the case for "Islam Pribumi: Menolak Arabisme, Mencari Islam Indonesia" ("Indigenous Islam: Rejecting Arabism, Seeking Indonesian Islam") recently explored in an Indonesian journal, *Tashwirul Afkar*, 14 (2003), co-published by the Asia Foundation. "Rejecting Arabism" in matters of religion need not, of course, imply antipathy toward Arabs per se.

[20] On regimist Islam, see Robert Hefner, *Civil Islam: Muslims and Democratization in Indonesia* (Princeton, NJ: Princeton University Press, 2000), p. 19 and ch. 6.

[21] In the Indonesian language, *masyarakat madani* is an Islam-tinged rendition of "civil society," whose secular translation is *masyarakat sipil*. Intriguing in this context is a recent volume, *Indonesia Kita* (Jakarta: Gramedia Pustaka Utama, 2004), by the dean of liberal Muslims in Indonesia, Nurcholish Madjid. Madjid begins by praising the system of rule established by the Prophet Muhammad in Medina in the 7th century as a suitable model for modern Indonesia. But at the end of the book, when he reaches the 21st century, he ignores the Medinan paradigm altogether. Instead he treats his country's current plight and what to do about it in almost entirely secular terms. For all his early extolling of Medinan rule, Madjid does not see in Islam a practical blueprint for the state. In his eyes, that project would only alienate moderate Muslims and non-Muslims. Islam is instead, for Madjid, an ethical outlook — a call to goodness and tolerance that any and all Indonesians can accept. By implication, as a basis for Indonesian identity, Islam's political failure is a necessary condition of its moral success.

8

Highlights
of
Discussion

I n the preceding chapters, our authors raised some major
questions and broached fresh ideas regarding the complexities
of the Islamic and Christian religions as they are played out in
the social fabrics of modern Indonesia and the Philippines. What
follows are edited excerpts from the group discussion as our experts
— scholars, religious leaders, activists — interacted among themselves
and with a warmly engaged audience. For the benefit of our readers,
we have organized these excerpts into major topics of discussion. – Ed.

New Islamic Institutions

Azyumardi Azra: We should note the rise of new
institutions like Islamic elite schools, Islamic
banks, Islamic insurance, and Islamic philanthropy

organizations. I have been asked by many journalists, particularly from the States, whether this development would lead to the transformation of Indonesia into an Islamic state. I usually react to this question by saying that this represents increased piety rather than increased Islamic politics among Indonesian Muslims. This argument can be supported by the fact that during and since the election of 1999, most Indonesian Muslims cast their vote not for Islamic parties but for secular parties, non-religious parties, like PDI-P and Golkar.

"Pancasila Should Be Revived"

Azyumardi Azra: The concept of Pancasila should be revived in my opinion. Of course, I do not like that Pancasila had been used, is used, or will be used as a tool for the maintenance of the political status quo. However, I believe Pancasila is among two or three of the remaining integrating factors of the Indonesian nation-state. So my argument is that Pancasila should be revived, should be rejuvenated and then should be made an open ideology, which means that the interpretation of Pancasila is open to any Indonesian citizen, not dominated by the state.

Opportunities Seized by Radical Islam

Azyumardi Azra: After the fall of Suharto, there were a number of reasons why radical groups became more and more obvious, especially before the Bali bombing:

- The political liberalization in Indonesia after the fall of Suharto allowed everybody, any group, to express themselves, including the radicals.
- The breakdown of law and order, and the disruption of Indonesian politics upon the fall of Suharto, which allowed other disintegrations to occur.
- The decline of central authority itself, while at the same time we also implemented a decentralization program.
- Political fragmentation among Indonesians. We had, for instance, 48 parties in the General Election of 1999. Then we still had 24 political parties participating in the parliamentary election of 2004. So, with this political fragmentation, each group, including of course the military, tries to recruit and use and abuse certain other groups within society for their own political purposes.
- The demoralization of law enforcement agencies, including the police. There has been bitter fighting between the police and the Indonesian military (TNI) because the TNI, according to the decree

by the People's Consultative Assembly, have to "return to the barracks." So their "dual function" has been abolished.

∎ Economic depression and economic crisis. Many who take to the street are in fact professional demonstrators. They get paid. They will hire out to certain groups.

∎ The abolishment of the anti-subversion law that had been used by the Suharto regime for his political purposes. Only after the Bali bombing of 2002 did the Indonesian Parliament and government introduce a new anti-terror program and anti-terrorist law.

Containing Radical Islam in the Future

Azyumardi Azra: Especially after the Bali and Marriott bombings in Jakarta, most of these radical groups have been lying low. Laskar Jihad has disbanded itself. Also, Front Pembela Islam. But these groups can be reactivated by their leadership if they feel that they have to do so. Therefore, I think there are some keys to countering such tendencies toward reactivation:

∎ Re-strengthening of law enforcement. This is very important, because if you have a vacuum in the enforcement of law and order, then these groups will take law into their own hands.

∎ Re-strengthening of the state. We need a strong state. Of course, I have to say that a "strong state" does not necessarily mean also an autocratic state. Or a military state. A democratic state should be a strong democratic state, like what you have in the USA.

∎ Empowering mainstream, moderate Muslim organizations. The NU and Muhammidiyah are very big organizations, but sometimes they are very slow because they are busy with daily routine activities. They have a lot of institutions: *pesantren, madrasah*, general schools, universities. But many of these educational institutions are in very bad condition. We need to empower these institutions.

∎ Consolidating and deepening of democracy. We cannot take democracy for granted. We have to develop it. For instance, my university for the last four years has introduced civic education. This is a required course. Civic education replaces a very militaristic course on Indonesian identity and Indonesian integrity.

∎ It is also important that democracies like the United States, for instance, give good examples of how democracy is practiced. If I can say it, some policies of the United States are counter-productive. By supporting undemocratic, military regimes, for instance. This is not a good example for us in Indonesia. And also taking all law into the United States' own hand. For instance, by going to war in Iraq. This is also not a good example for us.

Images of Christ, and Social Hierarchy

Cruz: In some Philippine towns and cities, images of the suffering or dead Christ are carried through the streets during Holy Week. The images are ordinarily kept in people's homes in storage, or even in living rooms; and I suggest that the sense of ease that people have of keeping the image of a dead person in their house is rooted, in part, in an earlier tradition, before the 16th century, where the leading family takes over the body of the dead leader for his secondary burial. So I suggest the contemporary practice of owning a religious image of the dead or suffering Christ is, at the same time, an act of devotion; but it's also an indicator of one's place in the social hierarchy. It's an example, I think, of how social forces shape society, and how society, in turn, shapes these forces, and in some measure, religion.

Political Choices: The Church and the Masses at Odds

Cruz: When the masses make political choices at variance with the published preferences of the Catholic Church, we might ask whether the Church may be rendering itself increasingly irrelevant. The civil disturbances of May 1, 2001, called by some EDSA III, or EDSA *Tres*, are instructive. In the early hours of that day, large crowds, crowds originating mainly from the slums of metro Manila, attacked the presidential palace in protest over Estrada's ouster and detention.

To the chagrin of the NGOs and many Church groups that had openly supported Estrada's impeachment, many of the protestors came from areas that had been under their care for years. What the Church groups found disconcerting was not so much the fact that their people had somehow moved over to the other side, but that their political action completely caught them by surprise. It was as if the Church had been out of touch with its own people.

The May 1, 2001 protest may be an omen of protests to come. The event revealed not only a growing desperation among the people, but also their alienation from their traditional leaders, among whom they count the Church. If the Church is unable to renew its presence among the masses and to articulate its response to their social concerns, a parting of ways may take place. Millions of Catholics, even now, take their cues *not* from Church officials, but from leaders like Mike Velarde and other charismatic figures whose links to the Church are tenuous. I speculate on why things are moving in this direction.

In the Philippines, Christianity's presence in the public sphere has typically been in a denunciatory mode, not in a constructive mode. The Church has shown itself capable of tearing things down, as it did in bankrupt administrations. But what it has not demonstrated is its capacity to build up, to sustain a campaign for productivity and equitability.

Weakness of Philippine State; Need for Church Vision and Action

Cruz: Not only is the Philippine state weak, I can make a strong case that it is getting weaker. The Chief Justice of the Supreme Court barely escaped impeachment; the President has had to balance good policy with being re-elected; Congress passed only a handful of significant legislation. The formal mechanisms of authority, I think, suffer from partial paralysis.

As the state shows itself increasingly unable to design and carry out a program of national reconstruction, the Church is being called to bring its vision and its resources to the project of rebuilding the country. But while the Church's position on family planning is well known, its position on agrarian reform, taxation, the environment, and other important issues is not fully articulated. The Church cannot hope to bring reform in these areas without wrestling with the formal mechanisms of civil authority. Should it succeed in awakening the considerable qualities and resources of the people, the Church then would have to grapple with the issue of its intervention in matters of state.

Indonesian Nationalism Is Multi-Confessional, Not Secular

Hefner: It is important, I think, not to attempt to locate the dynamics of state, society, and religion in Indonesia within the framework of secular nationalism. Indonesia is not, and really has never been, a secular-nationalist country; and the mainstream tradition of nationalism in Indonesia has never been secular nationalist. It is and has been, instead, multi-confessional, and religious in the sense that it recognizes that religion is a public good; and a good that should be supported by and enriched by the activities of state as well as society. But no single religion should be designated as the religion of state. So: a multi-confessional nationalism, not a secular nationalism.

"Sectarian Trawling" in Indonesia

Hefner: Beginning in the late 1980s and early 1990s, President Suharto himself authorized the establishment of an Islamist or Green Faction in the army forces, a body that had heretofore been a bastion of conservative multi-confessional nationalism. At this time also, moving very quickly, President Suharto attempted a series of co-optative outreaches to the two main Muslim organizations about which Pak Azyumardi talked, Nahdlatul Ulama and Muhammadiyah. They cooperated with the President for social and educational affairs; but when it came to politics, the Muslim leadership continued to press for political and democratic reforms, something that irritated President Suharto enormously.

So then, starting around 1993 or 1994, we begin to see an off-the-record but very systematic outreach, not just to Muslim radicals but to extremists, to armed groups and groups that are much more vehemently anti-Pancasila, anti-Christian, and anti-Western, than any Muslim groups with which Suharto had previously interacted. It was a pattern that I've called "sectarian trawling." That is, reaching into religious communities and actually trying to exacerbate religious tensions for your own political benefit. Suharto failed. The tactic, obviously in terms of his own short-term interests, didn't succeed. It wasn't enough to keep him in power.

Secularity and Mystery in Western Religion

Rafael: What you get with the notion of religion, at least in the Western context in which it has been deployed, certainly since Roman-Christian times, is this notion of a paradox. On the one hand, religion is necessarily productive of social life, the realm of the secular and the profane, which entails publicity, rationality, calculation. At the same time, this profane secular realm is founded on something beyond and before sociology. It is founded on mystery, infinity, the incalculable.

EDSAs I and II (1986, 2001): Excitement and Dread

Rafael: After addressing God through prayer, the people then sought to install figures from the old oligarchy: Cory at EDSA I, Gloria Macapagal-Arroyo at EDSA II. Faced with both the dread and the pleasure of uncertainty, they chose, as it were, to return to conventional notions of sociology. Thus, the religiosity of the first two EDSAs has a double aspect, contradicting while complementing one another. On the one hand, EDSA witnessed the unconditional hospitality for that which would come at the limits of knowledge and at the threshold of faith — the unknown, the impossible, the possibility of justice and freedom.

On the other hand, it also witnessed the popular *recoil* from this revolutionary possibility. This popular recoil characterizes so many moments of Philippine history. When confronted with the possibility of radical change, people turn around. They turn around. They search for a more comforting, more conventional, more livable form of authority, whether in religious or political terms. However, this tension remains unresolved. And it is this tension, I suggest, that gets played out every day and particularly during tumultuous moments [such as presidential elections and challenges to the presidency – *Ed.*].

Primordial Loyalties

Rocamora: In the case of both Indonesia and the Philippines, Islam is, and can be, a progressive force. It is a force that can be supportive of democracy and civility, and not at all of necessity supportive of terrorism and other

Fig. 31

Seminarians Against Estrada, Davao City. Extended impeachment charges against President Joseph "Erap" Estrada, on grounds of embezzlement and fraud, were obstructed short of conclusion in the Philippine Senate. Long-simmering public impatience took form in increasingly widespread demonstrations, as here in Mindanao, marching past San Pedro Cathedral, 19 January 2001. (Gene Boyd Lumanang, *Philippines Enquirer*)

Fig. 32

People Power Group at EDSA Shrine. The shrine built at a major intersection of Epifanio de los Santos Avenue (EDSA) to commemorate the triumph of democratic volunteerism (1986) became a natural focal point for those trying to unseat President Estrada and replace him with Vice President Gloria Macapagal Arroyo. Here, 20 January 2001, they assemble for a peaceful march on Malacanang Palace. (Mike Alquinto, *Philippines Enquirer*) The support of church, military, and business elements was vindicated by a Supreme Court opinion from Chief Justice Honor Davide. Estrada was put in detention, and Arroyo installed in office.

radical armed political expressions. I insert that proposition in the debates which have been going on in Indonesia in the last few years, on the restructuring of the Indonesian state, and the role of what are referred to in Indonesia as "primordial loyalties." In the discourse on political reform in Indonesia, I continually see primordial loyalties being placed on the side of bad things. Somehow, in the reconstruction of the Indonesian state, in particular in the design of new representative institutions, primordial loyalties should not be given very much room.

I've argued with friends in Indonesia about this. And I say to them, 'Well, what you referred to was primordial loyalties; and the kinds of social expression which historically have provided a strong social base for Indonesian political parties might not be as bad as you've made it out to be if you look at it from the vantage point of the Philippines, where political parties, for all intents and purposes, do not exist, precisely because they don't have primordial loyalties to base them on' — that's what I say to them.

Philippine Government Must Think of Islam Positively

Rocamora: Without taking sides in this old, old debate that will continue forever and ever, I would end simply by saying: maybe, if the central government in the Philippines could think of Islam in different ways, if they could think of Islam as a positive force in Moro social life — maybe it might be easier to deal with the problem of the so-called Moro insurgency in the south. And maybe for all of us, if we widen our understandings of the relationship between religion and politics, it might contribute to finding solutions to the problems generated by religion on politics and politics on religion.

Corruption of Political Language

Emmerson: There is, at some level I guess, an inescapable paradox: How do you talk about the absolute in relative terms without violating the terminology of the absolute? Or to reverse it, how can you talk absolutely about religion which is also, undeniably, a relativistic phenomenon?

We all have different views and different behaviors; and to be quite frank about it, not all Christians live up to the Ten Commandments. So you can't infer from high doctrine, daily behavior. Are these really Islamic militants that are throwing bombs? Are we to infer from that, that in the destruction that they create, they are, in fact, true to Islam? That's what, I think, we are being encouraged [by the media – *Ed*.] to think. And if this isn't Orwellian corruption of language that in fact inhibits our ability to think clearly, not to mention our ability to generate appropriate policy, I don't know what is.

Malaysia: Mahathir Outflanks the Islamists

Emmerson: Think of a triple-decker sandwich in which you have Society on the bottom, Nation intermediate, in the middle, and State on the top. Now the likelihood that Indonesia would become an Islamic state is, it seems to me, at the moment, infinitesimal. It is very hard to conceive of that unless, going back to my earlier point, you revise what you mean by an Islamic state. Now, that is exactly what has been happening across the Straits in Malaysia. Where, in a grand gesture of rhetorical co-optation, Mahathir Mohammed, before his departure, announced, "Well, we already *are* an Islamic state," and therefore PAS, the opposition party, that has a very different image and agenda, is outflanked.

Serious Engagement with Islam

Hefner: Don Emmerson is more optimistic than I am about the ability to circumvent serious engagement with Islam. And in particular I think if any

Fig. 33

Unveiling of Marker to EDSA Heroes. Former Presidents Aquino and Ramos, with Cardinal Sin, line up with new President Arroyo for further sanctification of political religiosity, 25 February 2001. (Lyn Rillon, *Philippines Enquirer*)

Full text of the *Marker to EDSA Heroes* appears on the following page ➤

ON THIS GROUND
Millions of indignant, vigilant, and black-clad Filipinos started
a vigil for moral renewal in public governance
on January 17, 2001
singing together, praying together,
chanting protest slogans together, and
charting together a new course
for the history of peaceful political change.
On this holy ground
at high noon on the 20th of January 2001, the eve of The Feast of
the Sto-Nino,
GLORIA MACAPAGAL ARROYO
was sworn in as the
fourteenth president of the Republic of the Philippines
under the shadow of Mary, our Lady of EDSA,
in the presence of millions of peace-loving Filipinos.
Henceforth
all generations to come
shall call this historical event as the
SECOND EDSA PEOPLE POWER REVOLUTION.
To the
UNNAMED FILIPINOS
whose love of God has
made that historical event come about
this
hallowed spot
is gratefully dedicated.

Muslim country is to strengthen its foundation for pluralism, democratic civility, and democratic citizenship, it has to be by way of very serious engagement by Muslims with Islam itself, rather than a gradual, loosening of commitment to Islamic ideals, and/or forgetting of the fact that 'oh, well, we're Muslims.'

I don't think that this has always been the case. One of the great, unexpected events of the 20th century was the Islamic resurgence that swept really all of the Muslim world, a resurgence that has women wearing *jilbab* or *hijab* in greater numbers in all Muslim societies, and a whole slew of other entailments ranging from how you eat to how you think about the political sphere. In the aftermath of this resurgence, I think it's hard to go back to the Youth Oath of 1928, with the principles that you so nicely and for me, too, so idealistically describe. To go back to them requires a much more significant detour through and into a sustained engagement by Muslims with Islamic rationales for pluralism, democracy, and citizenship.

Emmerson: [But] such a process of internal reform, to establish on a long-run basis, if I can put it this way, the *liberality* of Islam as thought and practiced in Indonesia, would be a logical prior step to what an outsider would call a secular situation. If you were an Indonesian politician running for office 60 years from now, you still would not say, 'I'm a secularist.' But for all practical purposes, the privatization of Islam, that one particular sort of *ijtihad* (interpretation), would be entirely compatible with that. But people still are reluctant to acknowledge that, because that could disinter all those skeletons I was talking about in my presentation.

Hefner: The outcome that you're describing is secular. But I maintain that the process will not be identical to that promoted by radical secularists, be they American or Indonesian.

Emmerson: I agree.

Hefner: And everything depends on the process. And on policy, formulating the right policies with USAID, with the US government, and with the German foundations working with Indonesians. Policy, I think, is a very serious issue and has to be taken seriously. The process of democratization, pluralization, and liberalization in the Muslim community isn't effectively achievable if you ignore Islam and the detailed arguments of Muslim intellectuals. You have to work through the educational system, through the State Islamic University, et cetera.

Modernity, Tolerance, and Theological Engineering

Cruz: My question is not too different from what Bob and Mardi have asked. In the phrase "secular Islam," modernity and tolerance and other fine things seem to be ascribed to *secularity* rather than *Islam*. And my question is: "Is there a variety of Islam that can be the source *precisely* of all these fine things?"

Friend: Superb question.

Emmerson: My political-religious science fiction could be from an ethnocentrically American point of view, wildly optimistic. Bob is absolutely right. Let me just allude to a portion of my paper, which I did not share, which is apocalyptic. That is to say, if "Under God" [in the Pledge of Allegiance – *Ed.*] was generated by Senator Ferguson, in the heat of the Cold War, as an effort to separate Americans from godless communism, it is entirely possible to imagine a clash of civilizations on a global scale, in which every Muslim country becomes, in effect, a front. And in which, therefore, inside Indonesia — given its concentration of Muslims — it is possible, in an exclusive manner, to find the majority saying, "You Christians, you're not part of this." Not to mention, of course, reversing and repealing the incredible theological engineering that led to the result that Hinduism is treated as monotheistic. And so you could imagine the insertion, maybe not of a phrase, "Under Islam," but of the equivalent in a very militant and damaging and intolerant interpretation of that first *sila* of Pancasila. Which at least fits with the argument I was trying to make as to the changeability of these circumstances.

It is true that we are on the downswing or plateau of a dramatic Islamic resurgence. If things wax, they can wane. Is it not conceivable that 20 or 30 years from now we would look back on that resurgence and say, 'Ah, how historically quaint. And look what happened afterwards...'?

US Government Must Stick to a Secular Agenda

Emmerson: Part of me says the US government should stay the hell out of theological reform. We have no comparative advantage there! We ought to try to involve ourselves in the things that we do reasonably well, a secular agenda: better education, economic development. And then *hope*, because it's only a hope, that somehow the militants will decline.

American Evangelicalism Across Two Centuries

Hefner: I think part of the difficulty that we have with thinking about secularity is that Americans, and I'll be too blunt here and too simplistic, but for the sake of being provocative, Americans misunderstand their own religious history. One of the things that has happened in the sociology of religion in the United States over the last 20 years is the recognition that this great myth of secularity assumes that there was progressive enlightenment.

And enlightenment meant privatization. And privatization meant that religion doesn't get involved in public issues. It doesn't, and it shouldn't be allowed to.

That is in effect a myth that seriously distorts not just what's happening now, but what happened in the 19th century. The great thing that liberal historians overlook in church history, Christian history in particular, is that really the most dramatic event in Christian America in the 19th century was the rise of evangelicalism. Not just as a theology, but as a social organization that from the 1820s-1830s on, became a theology that doesn't retreat. It continues its progressive expansion into vast portions of American society right up until today. The rise of evangelicals isn't a post-1960s phenomenon; it's a post-1830s phenomenon.

I think we must recognize that this type of process took place here in the United States. It didn't take place in France, didn't take place in most of Western Europe, but it did take place in the United States. I think this type of process is similar to what we're looking at in the Muslim world. What does that mean? That doesn't mean 90% of the Muslim populace in Muslim-majority countries hold unchanging to the same sets of religious doctrines, or even are all that pious. But it does mean that a significant constituency is here to stay.

This constituency takes religious ideas and the need to rationalize all programs — economic, political, including programs concerned with democracy and pluralism — in Islamic terms. We're looking at the Muslim world counterpart to the ascent of evangelical Christians in the United States. And rather than dismissing them as people who reflect an older era, a kind of living relic that's about to die, we have to say, 'No, no. That is part of our modern world. That's part of modern America and this is going to be something we have to engage in the Muslim world, sympathetically and seriously, just as we do in our own society.'

EDSA III: Failure and Revenge

Cruz: Let me just address a very narrow sliver of the issue and that is, what EDSA III has done is precisely to expose the failure of both EDSA I and II in bringing about social change. Now the fact that no widespread systemic reconfiguration has taken place cannot be explained by the event of May 1, 2001, EDSA III. But now I think it is in the consciousness of many decision-makers that an EDSA IV is a distinct possibility, and at that time, we may not be so lucky.

Rocamora: They even mispronounce it and say "EDSA For?"!

Rafael: I don't know what to say….I tried to come to terms with the aftermath of both EDSA I and EDSA II, and even EDSA III. I do talk about EDSA III in a separate work where I refer to it as unfolding according to a logic of revenge. The question of revenge is absolutely crucial, I believe, to understanding not just Philippine politics but I think many other political phenomena that we see today.

Vengeance first and foremost is a kind of historical reckoning. In many respects, revenge may perhaps be the most elementary experience of justice that's available to most people — people who have no access to courts, who have no access to police, who have no access to any kind of meaningful political participation. That's why revenge is always *sweet*. But it's always served *cold*. It's best served cold. As you know, Quentin Tarantino says. You *know*!

I think we need to take seriously the way in which revenge itself recapitulates a certain kind of Biblical logic, right? Very Old Testament. That's one way of thinking about EDSA III. It's very difficult to dismiss simply as populist manipulation or the manipulation of certain lumpenproletariat by interested parties, on the part of Estrada or Marcos and so forth. Ah, it is that. It's certainly that. But I think it also has to do with the sense in which people feel it provides them with the chance to take what they can.

Now, there is also an aspect of revenge that begins to shade into criminality. Criminality is the other looming topic here that hasn't been brought up. As Perry Anderson has said in another context, between revolution and hegemony, there is criminality. Criminality is that mediating point between radical social change and the simple reassertion of the status quo. There's always criminality.

Criminality, Inequality, Evangelicalism

Rafael: I'm not sure if you can say *nothing* has changed. Things always change. But the question is, why haven't they changed in the direction that we want them to change? I mean, the killers of Ninoy Aquino still haven't been prosecuted. The billions that Marcos has stolen still haven't been recuperated. Let's just start from there. This thing with Estrada probably will end in the same situation: no money will be restored. And even if the money were taken, as we've seen in the history — the sad, tragic history of the PCGG [Philippine Commission on Good Government] — the very people tasked with recuperating Marcos' wealth, themselves become corrupt. You know, it's like the cops who bust into a drug house and realize, 'Oh, there's all this money. Well, it's two million bucks here. I'll take a couple thousand. Nobody will miss it.' The kind of logic where the cops themselves become criminals.

I think the temptations of criminality are so strong, because there is no guarantee of justice. There is no access to justice as far as I'm concerned. Why have the EDSAs failed? Because the institutions of justice have failed.

It's not so much that the state is weak. The state is weak because the venues, the possibility of addressing injustice, are rather feeble. And so people go to Church, they pray. God is one way of doing it. I think one of the most interesting phenomenon in the Philippines now is the rise of born-again Christianity. Evangelical Christians. As Bob Hefner has said, this is an utterly global phenomenon and it cuts across classes. You have it among working classes, but it's also phenomenally true for upper classes. A lot of people I went to school with, for example, who ended up staying in the Philippines, some of them got rich — took advantage of pulling strings, particularly during the Ramos administration — and many of them have become born-again Christians. I think it's consistent with many things we see in places like Vietnam, in places like rural China and various other places where you have emergence of newly rich or new bourgeois people taking advantage of these entrepreneurial opportunities. They need to find a way to explain their wealth.

They need to find a way of making sense of the fact that, all of a sudden, there are these new configurations of inequality. And somehow they're on top and other people are below. How do you justify that? And the question of justifying wealth is precisely, directly related to the question of justice. Right? How do you justify inequality and still pretend that somehow you're living a *just* life? Well, I think born-again Christianity is a very, very seductive way of doing so. Evangelicalism is a very seductive way of saying, 'Well, justice not now, but certainly in the afterlife.' The idea that justice can be located somewhere else and that the situation of injustice that exists today, is not so much the result of socioeconomic arrangements, but in fact the result of certain kinds of moral states.

It's true here. It's true everywhere else. And that's sort of the argument you get: People are poor because they are sinful. Poverty is the result of some kind of moral decrepitude and has nothing to do with some sort of unequal distribution of resources, et cetera, et cetera, et cetera.

Misjudgments by Indonesian Hardline Radical Fringe

Hefner: Indonesia's hardline fringe, though very, very small, has shown consistently from the 1940s to the 1990s and 2000s, a unique ability to *misjudge* the political climate. And to misjudge the whole Muslim community, not just the middle class, but certainly the middle class as well.

It's an extraordinary miscalculation; one that is found in other societies, but the degree of irrealism and romanticization of violence that characterizes radical Islamists in Indonesia is really extraordinary. And again, I link it in part not just to Islam but to the tradition of *pemuda* violence and the sort of romanticization of violence that you see in Indonesia generally.

The Philippine National Democratic Front as Terrorist Force

Rocamora: A few years ago, when it hadn't been too long since I had left the underground myself, I declined to use the word "terrorist" on the National Democratic Front because the National Democratic Front had proximate, achievable political goals. In the five or six years since I made that judgment, I've turned around and said, well, now actually I think the NDF *should* be called a terrorist organization. I think that the underground Communist Party has lost touch with reality and that its political goals cannot, by any stretch of the imagination, any more be called proximate…and that's in terms of its extension into the future. If you take it back to the past, the way that the Communist Party is conducting itself at this point, in my opinion, is a perversion of the goals of that underground when it started 30 or more years ago. As you will see from the way that I use the word "terrorist," it's not an *etymological* explanation — I use it as a club.

Kaddafi Interventions; Absence of Trust

Rafael: Why can't there be a third party ostensibly with some kind of Muslim allegiance to mediate between the government and warring groups in Mindanao? Many people in this room work in that part of the region. Please correct me if I'm wrong. But my understanding of the history of the conflict is that in 1976, this is exactly what Marcos tried to do by encouraging Kaddafi to get actively involved in the negotiation with the MNLF at that time. What came out was the Tripoli Agreement, the terms of which weren't actually enacted until about 1996, during the Ramos administration. This is the point where ARM [Autonomous Region of Mindanao] was actually created, elections were conducted, and Nur Misuari ended up becoming Governor and for a while, as well, becoming a traditional Filipino politician, until he broke loose and went off his other way.

And, of course, Kaddafi had been historically involved with negotiations with the hostage crisis among the Abu Sayyaf — at least during the earlier parts of the crisis negotiation back in 2000, or maybe 1999. This was the first wave of Abu Sayyaf activities where Kaddafi intervened to the point of actually giving part of the ransom money to have some of the hostages released. So that has happened, but I don't think it's sustainable.

I think this is probably very simplistic, but something worth pondering about — there's no trust on both sides. You can't negotiate unless there's some trust on both sides. The Muslims in Mindanao have enormous amounts to complain about. And they have no one to turn to. They have no representation. There is no coherent body of Muslim political leaders that could intervene, that could help. The incredible brutality of the military in Mindanao cannot be underestimated. And it's precisely what drives people into these organizations. And it's what feeds fantasies of revenge that, again, feed the violence. So I think, the *fundamental question* is trust.

No Justice for Filipino Muslims

Rafael: I couldn't help reacting when you said, "There is no justice there." You know that saying, "There is no justice, there's JUST US." Every economic indicator shows just how impoverished the Muslim population is in the area; and if you look at the Muslim population in Quiapo in Manila itself, which originally Marcos had put up in order to showcase the martial law regime's benevolence towards its minorities...I mean, they're basically slums. Basically slums. They've been incorporated into the rest of the Manila slums. It's really pathetic.

The poverty, plus the incredibly entrenched prejudice of Christian settlers in those areas, the incredible racism against Muslims, this is something that Christian Filipinos have never, never come to terms with. So you've got the racism, you've got the poverty, you've got the military brutality. You've got total distrust in the government. You've got corruption among the local leaders. I don't even know where to begin.

You can't work in the old 1980s-1990s paradigm of seeing the state and civil society as engaged in a zero-sum game, so that when the state wins, civil society loses. No, the essence of democracy is a certain type of strong state that strengthens pluralist and democratic institutions, traditions, and groupings in society, and in so doing, hopefully, develops public culture. Thereby both of these sides of the democratic coin are themselves reinforced but [both state and civil society are] also guarded against, lest they lose their way.

State and Civil Society: Not Opposed, but Cooperative

Hefner: Exactly right. That is, you want to scale up the social capacities of certain bureaus, departments, and agencies in the state, particularly those that interface with civic, pluralist, democratic-minded people in groupings and organizations in society. Suharto didn't do this; he did the opposite.

Whatever his achievements in economic development and education and other spheres, certainly, one of the saddest legacies of the Suharto era was how, during the last 12 years of his administration, he not only neglected this great reservoir of good-minded democratic capital, but he abused it when he realized it was challenging him. So the key is to develop institutions.

Atrophy of Church Reform; Desecration of EDSA Shrine

Audience: My question is directed mostly to Father Cruz, but also to Joel. Those of us who have followed the Philippines for a while have often looked to the Catholic Church as a unifying, stabilizing force and, certainly since the late Marcos era and into the late 1980s, a force for some degree of political and social change. But you've presented, as I've understood it, a picture of a Church that may have atrophied with regard to its political and social reform agenda. If that is in fact the case, why? And what might be done about it? And more specifically, it also raises the question of should there be religious political parties in the Philippines?

Friend: OK, what is the political reform agenda? Should there be religious political parties? Brief comments, from Joey, and from Joel.

Cruz: I think there has always been social thought within the Catholic Church represented by the papal encyclicals. But also locally grown articulation of what ought to be. What I was simply underscoring was the fact that I think the Catholic Church, in part because of the decrease of the clergy, and by extension the decrease in liturgical life, is slowly losing its ability to translate that social vision into reality.

There are segments of the Church that continue to think of what changes ought to be, but the Church is losing its ability to implement these changes. That is represented by withdrawal from poor communities and the rise of alternative groupings, other Christian churches, and the overseas migration of 8 million Filipinos who are exposed to all sorts of religious traditions. The Philippines, I think, is best understood as part of a larger whole. The Church is increasingly losing its ability to influence events; it no longer acts in a hermetically sealed situation as it used to be.

Rocamora: Majority religions have difficulty translating themselves into significant political forces. If you look at Indonesia, Muslims complain about the fact that Islam does not play a more significant role in Indonesian politics than it has since independence. But I would suggest that precisely the reason for this difficulty is because it *is* a majority religion. Political expressions require differentiation: discourse on whether Megawati went to Mecca for religious purposes or political ones is just a non-starter. I mean, it doesn't work, politically. I would submit that the same thing is also at work in the Philippines. Precisely because Roman Catholicism is the majority religion in the Philippines, it would be difficult to build a political party around that expression of faith.

What has been tried in the past is differentiation by identifying with one distinct element in the tradition of Roman Catholicism, which is identification with the poor. Just why that identification lapsed, I'm not quite sure.

One indication might be found at the site where EDSA I, II, and III now have a shrine — which irreligious people like me refer to as 'The Shrine of Our Lady of the Flyover.' But what really struck me is, after EDSA III, Cardinal Sin prohibited political rallies at the EDSA Shrine. One of the few times I have made public theological statements was in protest to that decision. I said, "Cardinal, the sacredness of the EDSA Shrine has precisely to do with the people who made it what it is. And if you prohibit people from going there, then it loses its reason for being."

And what's even sadder is the way in which the desecration of the shrine was done...expressed in terms of unhappiness over the fact that, unlike the EDSA II crowd, the EDSA III crowd pissed all over the EDSA Shrine. Which brings me back to an expression from Black America to the effect that, "Life is a shit sandwich. The more bread you got, the less shit you gotta' eat." [Laughter]

Changing Views of Christian Engagement

Audience: It interests me that we are dealing with two countries with a majority religion and that we have spent a great deal of time talking, in relation to the Philippines, not in terms of the tensions within the majority religion, but in terms of the tension with the minority religion and the real troubles that causes. I would like particularly Father Cruz, but perhaps also Joel Rocamora, to talk about the tensions within the Church, and to expand further on the growth of evangelical religion both within the Catholic Church and within the wider community.

Cruz: Within the Christian groups there are strains that are either uncomfortable, unwilling, or uninterested in engaging the world as presently formulated. They think that Christianity is a spirituality of flight, and that its holiness is achieved precisely when one takes one's person outside of the dirty world. And I think the tension, or a tension, within Christianity, is precisely that which exists between those who think that holiness takes that form, and those who think that engagement with the world is precisely the arena in which to be truly Christian.

Friend: Thanks, Joey. Forgive me for intruding a quotation from Gandhi: "The path to holiness lies through action." Joel?

Rocamora: Let me try to answer the question with anecdotes. In a meeting between the government panel and the NDF in Oslo — the panel being of clerical fascists, because they're people who come out of what we on the left call the *sok dem* trend in the Philippine left. When one of these people who are accused complained about this tone, I said, "I have a very simple answer. Louie Jalandoni [vice chairman, NDF], being an ex-priest, was the original clerical Fascist." [Laughter] But the second anecdote has to do with an attempt that we at our institute [Institute for Popular Democracy] have made to try to get progressive Church people precisely to ask the kinds of questions that you've been asking us, Joey, which is, "What happened? What happened to the left in the Church?"

I'm the wrong person to encourage it, but so far, the only progress that we can claim is the fact that the distinction that Philippine progressives used to make between national democrats in the Church left, and so-called social democrats in the Church left, *is gone*. In other words, at least in the circles of Church people that I relate to, that kind of distinction doesn't exist any more. And I think that's a significant step. Because it means a redefinition of the categories within which the left thinks of itself and its political tasks.

Materialism, Development, and "Equal Opportunity" Policies

Hefner: I don't think that an overwhelming emphasis on economic growth had anything really to do with the fact that Suharto was a proponent of a conservative variant of multi-confessional nationalism. I just think it reflected, basically, the political economy of New Order Indonesia. And yet at the same time, I think some of the people who were committed to multi-confessional nationalism in the Suharto era believed in it quite genuinely, and many still do.

Emmerson: The missing argument that occurs to me would run something as follows: Let's try to detach this a little bit from the personality and human rights record of Suharto. Let's just think a little more abstractly. In a multi-confessional nationalism, there is present in the prefix 'multi' a constant, implicit tension between the components that are cobbled together in that prefix, 'multi,' and there is, therefore, a threat of destabilization, of conflict, of civil war.

Now, it therefore follows that among the solutions to this ongoing kind of structural tension would be one in which development, *pembangunan*, the preoccupation with material growth, would constitute a positive-sum arrangement where, even though one community's slice of the pie is smaller than another community, if we can keep the pie expanding, then radically destabilizing consequences can be kept in check. In a uni-confessional nationalism, this particular issue at least does not arise.

Take a look at Manila's response to Muslim Mindanao. Counter-insurgency plays the economic game, ubiquitously and repeatedly, in human history. The implicit logic is still there: that people don't live by bread alone, but as Joel just pointed out, it helps to be able to have bread.

Hefner: This is a materialist view of politics with which I strongly disagree, not because I'm anti-materialist, but because it's the wrong materialism. If you look at the history of the Islamic resurgence, not just in Indonesia but all around the world, some of its strongest carriers come from the middle class. It is a fact of the contemporary sociology of Islam and of the Islamic resurgence, that some of its most buoyant carriers are people from the middle class. People who precisely are no longer having difficulty satisfying the need for bread.

Emmerson: You're not saying that materialism breeds intolerance?

Hefner: No.

Emmerson: OK. I'm trying to defend an intriguing thesis. In Malaysia, you have a multi-confessional situation, which is also, not coincidentally, multi-ethnic. Is it coincidental that Malaysia has registered a rather impressive rate of economic growth? That whatever else you might think about Mahathir, he has precisely tried to engender this notion of a new Malay, a new Muslim Malay, a new middle class Muslim Malay, who might be less inclined to turn against a neighbor who happened to differ ethnically or religiously. Now, I don't want to develop this into some kind of law. The proposition does seem to me appealing — [to consider that "equal opportunity" policies for the majority may work well in the multi-ethnic, multi-confessional state – *Ed.*].

Tensions as Handled by Parish Priests

Friend: I think the [audience] question implies a deficit of social concern in the Catholic Church at present, registered hierarchically, if I heard right, from the top down. From the Pope, through the Cardinalate, through hierarchy in the Philippines, into parish priests. And he's asking, is that observation correct in your view and what can be done about it? Is that roughly so?

Audience: And it's also doctrinally: are the parish priests more interested in social justice, and are they not able to express that because of opinion that is coming down from higher within the Catholic Church?

Cruz: There is a very wide variety of perspectives even among parish priests. Even generationally you'd expect the younger ones to be more progressive but, in fact, we find in some cases the most dramatic conservatism among the very young. On the question, for instance, of population control, while the official Church teaching is pro-life, many parish priests in fact exercise or emphasize conscience in the formation of the decision. And this is understood by many as a practical sort of negation, if one can put it that way, of the official Church teaching. They are not outrightly opposing the Church, but in practice they give people a way out; I mean, some option. There is some tension, but the tension is not played out in public.

Islam and Civil Society in Malaysia

Emmerson: I think there is a tremendous irony in Malaysia, which is that Mahathir's strategy of co-opting Islam, out-flanking Islam, has generated what amounts to an incredibly conservative official religion, what Bob Hefner would call "regimist Islam" — including a religious bureaucracy. The Pusat Islam is a good illustration, and the Islamic University is another good example. So when we take, say, the track record of a group like Sisters in Islam (when they started out they were eight women), they have done, from my own point of view, heroic work in trying to spin the Koran towards feminism.

What have they accomplished? Perhaps my colleagues on the panel would be less pessimistic than I am, but unfortunately, I would have to say, not a great deal. For example, a number of commentators, including Patricia Martinez, a non-Muslim expert on Malaysian Islam, were accused of offending the religion. This became quite serious, because at the level of a *mufti*, at the state level, which is where religion is located, some rather dire things could have occurred to people who in my judgment are simply innocent.

And the irony is that the rescuer of these individuals did not come from some progressive Islamic overlay that had been cultivated and had engaged in seminars and *ijtihad* and gone that particular route. No, it was Mahathir. It was only Mahathir. Without the concentration of power in the hands of the Prime Minister, given the federal structure of Malaysia, things could have been a lot worse. I think that is both ironic and an indication of failure.

Hefner: I agree with Don, but I'm still bullish on Malaysia and on Malaysian Islam. I agree entirely that the mass-based civic organizations and democratically reformist organizations that exist and in fact thrive in the Muslim community of Indonesia, have almost no counterpart in Malaysia.

I don't blame Mahathir as massively as you do. His daughter, remember, was one of the supporters of Sisters in Islam, and Zaina Anwar, the current president of Sisters in Islam, has met with Mahathir on many occasions, and appealed to him, so it's a vulnerable strategy. Very different from Indonesia in the sense that Sisters in Islam actually has had significant influence. But only in as much as that influence is mediated through these very, very, personal, individualized ties. That means that there isn't the mass-based counterpart that you have in Indonesia. And it's not just numbers. In Indonesia, you have this ground swell of scholars and of institutions, like Pak Azyumardi's State Islamic University, that are there to raise their voices when people call for the apostate, or the person who's regarded as deviationist, to be punished or killed. Which, of course, does happen in Indonesia; but then, as you say, Don, the contrast in responses is striking.

Now, all that said, why would I be optimistic? Because I think that the blame for the conservatism actually lies in Malaysian society as much as it does in the state. Mahathir would have been, I believe, quite happy to promote a much more, not democratically progressive, but culturally pluralistic understanding of Islam, had he not had to out-flank Islamist opposition, which was much more conservative than its mainstream counterpart in Indonesia. So he was compelled to go with what society offered.

Society is changing — finally. That's where my optimism emerges. Society is changing. And education and the pluralization of the Muslim community in Malaysia are taking place. It's still got a long way to go. But the relaxation of this opposition antagonism between Chinese and Malays will have a great pluralizing influence on the Malay community as a whole. The Malay community has been constricted by this sense of having to maintain solidarity in the face of the Chinese community that's just damn good at business, education, and everything.

Azyumardi Azra: I think there are two things here. First of all, in Malaysia you don't have, like Bob just mentioned, mediating and bridging. So PAS and UMNO have been involved in a very bitter contest to dominate the interpretation of Islam. There is no middle ground.

The second difference from Indonesia in Malaysia is that Islam has been co-opted officially. In Malaysia, functionaries of Islam almost anywhere in society get paid by the government. [In some other Muslim nations, too, not inhibited by so-called separation of church and state, government salaries to Islamic functionaries have grown up unchallenged. – Ed.]

In Indonesia, you know, any sermon-giver can give anything he wants to give to the *jamaah*, to the audience, to the congregation. This is, of course, very historical. In Malaysia, the British basically maintained the status quo of the Sultan, the Ruler, over Islam. While in Indonesia, the Dutch abolished the Sultanates. This is, I think, a blessing in disguise for us in Indonesia, because we cannot be co-opted by the state. Muhammadiyah and NU are very independent. So what we need to do is to prevent these two organizations, Muhammadiyah and NU, from being involved in politics. If they get involved, then we are going to lose.

Developmentalism as a Religious Faith

Rafael: Right. I think it's a very appropriate question. It goes back to an earlier question about economic development. Developmentalism is precisely a kind of religious faith. And you have to believe that putting in roads, bridges, schools, and health care are going to improve people's lives. You have to believe that they're going to go along with what you're doing. You have to make them believe that you believe, right? In other words, developmentalism is every bit a kind of religious faith.

The Spectre of Death Feeds Reactionary Religiosity

Rafael: Now at this particular juncture, what are the possibilities for these kinds of radical changes? I don't know. I think this is why the question of terror is so relevant right now, because real change, radical change, always brings to mind, of course, revolution. During the period after Japanese occupation, revolutions were everywhere. And in the Philippines, of course, even before that. At also the turn of the century, right?

It's almost as if you were asking the question: 'What are the possibilities for revolutionary change?' At the moment, I just don't see the existence of revolutionary language, or a revolutionary vocabulary that might begin to guide people towards this kind of revolutionary change. Instead, what takes the place of revolutionary language, is a certain kind of *reactionary religiosity*. Yeah: evangelicalism, Islamism, whatever you want to call it, their claim to radicalness is precisely, I think, their ability to raise the spectre of terror.

I don't think any particular religion has a monopoly on that. The question of radical change is always connected, I think, to a frightful prospect of becoming other than who you are. And that always raises the spectre of death. Certainly in the case of the Philippines this is one of the reasons why you have a return to the Older Order, why you have the persistence, the incredible recalcitrance of these conservative forms. People are afraid. People are afraid.

And there is a certain kind of structural terrorism, if you will, that's in play, that keeps people in line. One of the first things it does is to impoverish the imagination. When you have an impoverished imagination, rather than thinking beyond existing parameters, what you end up doing is simply to reiterate what's given to you and then to toe the line. A rejoinder to Joey's observation earlier about the conservatism of the younger clergy is that, in fairness to them, the resources for thinking otherwise have become smaller and smaller.

Progressive Islam

Emmerson: There is such a thing as progressive Islam, as a concept that is being promoted. One wishes that there were millions lining up in a queue to join. Their rhetoric and their language are radically different from what we read in *The Washington Post*. Instead of terrorism, they talk about the *mustakbirun*, which means the *arrogant* — including the arrogance of the United States. They talk about the *mustadh'afin*, which means *the oppressed, the exploited*. They talk about *justice*. If there are single words that distinguish American discourse from Islamist discourse, they are, on the American side 'liberty,' and on the Islamist side, 'justice.'

Remember the days of liberation theology? We ought not to overlook that there are at least elements of this discourse within the Muslim world. Maybe that's hope, I don't know.

Indonesian Protestant Leaders Suspicious of Confucianism

Audience: Professor Azra, on the issue of multi-confessionalism and the virtually non-existent Confucianism in Indonesia, could you explain the national celebration of the Chinese New Year recently? Is it a sign of religious tolerance or is it a political or diplomatic move?

Azyumardi Azra: Only after President Abdurrahman Wahid was the celebration of things Chinese restored; public celebrations like Chinese New Year, for instance. Now, the leaders of Confucianism actually have been trying to get official recognition from the time of President Wahid. In fact, President Wahid promised to give that kind of recognition. But he failed to give it because there has been strong opposition from leaders from other religions. Particularly, if I'm not mistaken, from circles of Protestants.

Because Confucianism was regarded and declared by the Suharto regime as a kind of suppressive ideology, many Chinese converted to or adhered to Protestantism; and of course some of them also became Catholics. But now the recognition of Confucianism has been opposed by these Christian leaders, because if Confucianism is recognized, then these Chinese Christians are going to return to their original religion. So this is the problem. There is some kind of tug-of-war between Confucianism, its leaders, and the Christian Church leaders in Indonesia. At my university, we always invite leaders of Confucianism in religious dialogue or social dialogue on religion.

No brief summary of this discussion is possible. But the foregoing excerpts may illustrate that conceiving of Phil-Indo as one archipelago with two majority religions opens new doors of inquiry, and provides many corridors of discovery.

Multi-confessionalism in Indonesia may sometimes appear to be a form of state religiosity, which while holding the polity together satisfies neither creedal absolutists nor pragmatic seekers of social justice. Electoral democracy, however, appears presently reaffirmed.

Filipino disenchantment over a mono-religious system coexistent with serious failings of the state has given rise to recent national crises. EDSAs I and II were characterized by intense religiosity and reversion to pre-existing order. EDSA III was flavored with anti-establishment revenge against both socio-political order and the middle-class religiosity which had supported it. In years since, systemic failings remain unaddressed and a new crisis emerged in 2005 with constitutional flaws and class tensions evident. – Ed.

9

Religion and Religiosity in Phil-Indo

Theodore Friend

Everywhere religious icons and idioms can serve political ends, and political resources may be mobilized for religious ends. Indonesia and the Philippines are not exceptions. Islam and Christianity there, like all religions, are part of their surrounding social problems, and also, potentially, a very large part of their solutions. But, as our authors show, the Malay world is different from some parts of the world in neutralizing secularism. It continues in high degree to maintain societies with religious texture, states with religious tone, and moods of religious hope, with relatively few excesses of puritanism or of absolutism.[1]

In this context, Osama bin Laden's murderous *fatwa* (1998) against "Crusaders and Jews" appears not only barbaric, but strangely anachronistic. The military phase of the Crusades (1095-1291 C.E.) is more than seven hundred years past. Crusading is long gone as a psychic mainspring of Europe, but the past recoils upon it, as when terrorists killed 191 commuters in Madrid, 11 March 2004. A year later the Islamic Commission of Spain put out a reasoned Qur'anic answer to bin Ladenism and Al Qaeda, to solo decrees, extremist pretensions, and murderous suicides. These have no justification in Islam; they are prohibited and condemned. Their propagators and perpetrators are not Muslims at all, but *kafir murtad*, apostates and horrible malefactors outside of Islam altogether.[2]

By the year that the Muslim Ottomans were defeated outside Vienna, 1683, Islam had been peacefully percolating into Southeast Asia for centuries. The Dutch and Spanish in their mercantile expansion had established relatively new possessions for the sake of trade in the great archipelago of the Southwest Pacific. A ragged cleavage of their dominions existed between south of Mindanao and north of Borneo. Slow absorptive conquest and Christian missionary activity would eventually leave the approximate religious demography found today: nearly 90% Muslim and less than 10% Christian in the Republic of Indonesia; more than 90% Christian and much less than 10% Muslim in the Republic of the Philippines.

Half a world away from Amsterdam, Rome, and Mecca, the ugly half-brothers known as "crusade" and "jihad" have never dominated archipelagic psychology. Occasional neighborhood rumbles in Maluku and Mindanao may make the newspapers for sensation, but will not affect history books with significance. These outbreaks are at most faintly connected to bin Ladenism or to Bush-Blairism. They are largely local tangles of Islamo-fascists with Christo-fascists, or the product of vengeful opportunities on both sides.

In Phil-Indo, therefore, modern social morphology becomes of more moment to us than fading zigzag lines of historical causation. We see that the whole Malay world, in the course of its modern development, has taken the sting out of Western secularism. The sacred schism of the American, French, and Russian revolutions, that which separates state and church, has been found less than relevant. It has been sealed over in Malaysia, and glazed over with multi-confessionalism in Indonesia. In the Philippines, the organizational prominence of the Roman Catholic Church stimulates dodges from the separation principles. Deficits of both church and society lead to attempts to elevate both with strenuous religiosity.

---

[1] A generally helpful work is Andrew Willford and Kenneth M. George, eds., *Spirited Politics: Religion and Public Life in Contemporary Southeast Asia* (Ithaca, NY: Cornell University Southeast Asia Program Publications, 2005).

[2] Aljazeera.net, 13 March 2005. Full text of the *fatwa* appears in *The American Muslim*, January-March 2005 issue, updated 19 April 05.

If the "master narrative of secularization" has been confounded in the Malay world, we may well ask what counter-narrative — replacement, overwrite, or original — is unfolding there. What is its promise for those whose lives unfold within it? Not easy to see; hard to summarize. Perhaps it is a series of *hikayat*, traditional tales, peculiar and episodic. Perhaps all time should be seen as a series of cycles, in which the Western intrusions are merely embraced for taste, while the cycles, *masa perédaran* that enclose their ingredients, continue to unfold in their own inevitable but unpredictable rhythms. It might be wise to say that we simply do not know. It is well to have convictions about happenings within our own lifespans, and even passionate notions on what must be done. But on how it will all turn out, we ought better to be agnostic, and ready to enjoy the taste of comic surprise.

Western social science, however, and Western narrative art as well, hunger for specifics; and for particulars that suggest a future even while trying to contain the hubris that desires to know it. We have therefore employed three conceptual nouns for ourselves to use in gathering essayistic thoughts: state, society, and creed. What to make of them now? They cannot be bundled and rolled together in the way local governance, local habit, and local ritual are tightly wrapped among the Ifugao of Northern Luzon, or the Toraja of Central Sulawesi. The latter see their governance, religion, and culture as "round as the sun and the moon." But the scale of Phil-Indo is too grand for that. There are many handles, and many hands reaching for them. Things protrude at angles.

How, then, take hold? Francis Fukuyama is surely right to suggest that, globally considered, "the withering away of the state is not a prelude to utopia but to disaster."[3] The multiplication of failed states breeds misery and terrorism. Constructing state institutions is important, not only for international security, but for fundamental human welfare. This is true both within borders and, to the degrees that institutions may be implantable elsewhere, beyond them. Yes, "certain kinds of states, driven by utopian plans and an authoritarian disregard for the values, desires, and objections of their subjects, are indeed a mortal threat to human well-being."[4] And yes, also: Southeast Asia, Malay and other, has its own ways of making states, producing "transformations that have allowed incongruities to coexist, but also to merge."[5] Conceding all that, however, does not allow us to cherish states that

---

[3] Francis Fukuyama, *State-Building: Governance and World Order in the 21ˢᵗ Century* (Ithaca, NY: Cornell University Press, 2004), p. 120.

[4] James C. Scott, *Seeing Like a State: How Certain Schemes to Improve the Human Condition Have Failed* (New Haven and London: Yale University Press, 1998), p. 7.

[5] Tony Day, *Fluid Iron: State Formation in Southeast Asia* (Honolulu: University of Hawaii Press, 2002), p. 293

are routinely exploitative, absurdly "beautiful," superficially "talismanic," or routinely murderous. Mega-teleology alone does not justify a state. Far less will momentary ritual beauty do so. Our authors know that values, ends, and means must be weighed in many combinations and contexts, so they don't bother to say it. The editor, however, may mention it to encourage our guest, the reader, to move from the idea of state to the idea of society.

"Civil society" is a term dear to contemporary meliorists, who think progress can be got that way, incrementally or with millennial measures. Robert Putnam, popular arch-theorist in the matter, tracks the gains in well-being and self-respect of northern Italy over southern Italy across ten centuries.[6] He induces us not to be impatient to see the Mezzogiorno catch up with Tuscany, but willing, nonetheless, to urge the former to imitate the latter.

Lest we turn to Phil-Indo, however, with a see-all, solve-all civil society solution, multiplying NGOs and thereby maximizing imagined progress, let me enter two teasing examples as caveats. Where did Mussolini's fascism come from? North Italy and its dynamics, which unleashed more and other than the glories of social compacts. How did modern Spanish democracy arise? Out of Franco's dictatorship. Out of political institutions that he latterly allowed, and with minimal aid from civil society apparatus. In the Italian case, civil society was ineffective against fascism; in the Spanish case, irrelevant to democracy. History is slippery in these ways. Reach into the dark of its peddler's pack, and you're not sure what your hand draws out.

We have chosen to let our focus linger on religion and religiosity because some of us feel that social science has too easily despised the form of the first and amorphousness of the second. At the same time, we avoid the pseudo-dialectic of Islam vs. Christendom. We reject that angle as obsessive and deformed. Jerry Falwell is a grotesque counter-mimic of Osama when he says that "Islamic fundamentalists, radical terrorists, Middle Eastern monsters" wish to conquer the world; and apropos 9-11-01, that they had the help of Americans who brought disaster on themselves: "the pagans and the abortionists and the feminists and the gays and the lesbians….all of them who try to secularize America."[7]

Our essays, however, are not about the USA (280 million people) or about the Arabs (280 million people). They are about Phil-Indo (330 million people) in its local and global settings. They are about the ways that religion serves as a mold of culture; a stabilizer of personalities; a motivator of characters; an inspiration to societies; a monitor of states. Christianity and Islam do all these things in the Philippines and in Indonesia. And where

---

[6] Robert D. Putnam, *Making Democracy Work: Civic Traditions in Modern Italy* (Princeton, NJ: Princeton University Press, 1993).

[7] http://www.truthorfiction.com/rumors/f/falwell-robertson-wtc.htm.

they do not, religiosity springs up to attempt what ecclesiasts and imams cannot pull off.

The Philippines is not in the least *laïque* in the way that France is. The Philippines has not separated church and state nearly as fully as its model in that matter, the USA. In fact, their church from crisis to crisis may be tempted to correct the state, and between crises as well. Our writers suggest that it ought instead to be engaging with the state to improve society. Another writer goes further. Fr. John J. Carroll, S.J., sees EDSA III as spotlighting the wall of separation in Philippine society which protects the comfortable, including many churchpeople, from the desperately poor. "Until that wall is breached, Philippine democracy will remain a fraud."[8]

*

Indonesia as a secular republic is vastly different from Turkey. Indonesia is also very differently multi-confessional from Russia, which recognizes four primary faiths: Orthodox Catholicism, Islam, Judaism, and Buddhism. In Russia these represent a bag of creeds, jostling along with others, and with a widespread atheism that is, or will be, perhaps communism's most lasting product there. But in Indonesia atheism is interdicted. The allowable confessions are a plenum of beliefs, continuing strongly to shape the society. Having five faiths, and requiring concessions from tribal religions such as the Dayak and the Torajan that they fit in categorically, produces a kind of state religiosity rather than a sovereign dogmatism. Such a continuous religiosity *in the state* contrasts with the Philippines, where in 1986 and in 2001 especially, religiosity *in citizens* surged to reform the state or at least replace its president.

In 2004, Phil-Indo had major elections neither commandingly shaped by religion nor significantly tilted by religiosity. Indonesia held (for the first time) a second consecutive full, free, and fair national election; and, also for the first time, a direct presidential election. The winner, Gen. Susilo Bambang Yudhoyono, maintained a Muslim identity palpable enough to be acceptable without being to anyone offensive. For the electorate, apparently, his international perspective strengthened, by softening, his military credentials; and his clean record gave him voter-power in a notoriously corrupt political economy. In the year since his election, he has proven to be the first Indonesian president acting seriously to contain corruption. In Turkey, meanwhile, the army stands ready to rebuke or depose the carefully Islamist AK Party government elected late in 2002. At the insistence of the

---

[8] "Cracks in the Wall of Separation? The Church, Civil Society, and the State in the Philippines," in Lee Hock Guan, ed., *Civil Society in Southeast Asia* (Singapore: Institute of Southeast Asian Studies, 2004), pp. 54-77, quotation, p. 76.

constitutional court, the preceding Welfare Party and the Virtue Party were declared illegal for Islamic over-leanings. Without a massive shift of energies, Indonesia will not come close to such a situation. It will remain multi-confessional and Muslim-dominated with religiosity from microsegments — extremes of purity from *salafis*, and of violence from jihadists.

Meanwhile, in the Philippines, the electorate in 2004 conveyed a full six-year term as president to Gloria Macapagal Arroyo, who had served three years following the impeachment of her predecessor. Her margin of victory over Fernando Poe, Jr., about three percent in a field of five candidates, was complicated by charges of vote fraud on both sides. Poe's charges, after his premature death, were dismissed by the Supreme Court without examination of their merits. Arroyo, in her inaugural address, aimed to reconcile the three EDSAs rhetorically, and to proceed beyond them. But continuous newspaper speculation about plots and coups showed the political vascular system of the Philippines to be full of clots and plaque.

In the middle of 2005, tangible evidence surfaced that President Arroyo, the year before, had repeatedly phoned an election commissioner to ensure a secure margin of victory. Moods of sullen despair to active outrage followed. Arroyo played out a repertoire of defensive cards, holding legislative majorities as trump against impeachment. Cory Aquino asked the president to resign, but she would not. Eddie Ramos called for a change of system to clear the air and the political playing table. Many demonstrated in protest, but "EDSA fatigue" was noticeable. The Philippines, in August 2005, seemed resigned to constitutionality rather than elated with religiosity. There remained, however, possibilities of creeping impeachment or leaping coup. A slow burn was in process, with capacities either to fizzle out or explode. Three EDSAs and a mass vigil at the EDSA shrine as recently as the Oakwood Mutiny of 2003 had left Manilenos tired. But the Philippine capacity for religiosity in public life remained profound.

*

Two years before he died in 2005, Luis Taruc, the former Huk supremo, criticized President Arroyo on her way of accepting American military assistance against Islamic terrorism: "Why did you [indicate] the country is accepting Bush with open arms; why did you not say I accept you also with open legs[?]"[9] The former leader of socialist/communist rebels against the government in the 1940s and 1950s, Taruc spent over sixteen years in prison. When freed, he joined the Marcos of the early 1970s who was promising massive land reform. Again bitterly disappointed in his hopes for Filipino peasants and ordinary people, he swam his own way through the tides of the

---

[9] Tonette Martel, "Solo: Luis Taruc," *The Philippine Sunday Star*, 16 Feb 03, pp. H1-3, quotation, p. 3.

three EDSAs, his experience keeping him below elation and above despair. Reflecting on the Philippine history of the last century drew him back to Jose Rizal, the noble-hearted ilustrado executed by the Spanish in 1896. A thousand Huk veterans and farmers gathered with him under mango trees to celebrate his 91st birthday along with Rizal's birthday, and, as Luis put it, to celebrate the martyrdoms of many other ordinary Joses. Of himself, he wrote to me: "I'm just a bit player in the sad historical drama of my Motherland." Never a dogmatic Marxist, Taruc illustrated across many decades of colonial, post-colonial, dictatorial, and post-Marcos rule that his country had class divisions without class consciousness. Filipino religiosity, with its power to sublimate anger, was perhaps an underlying explanation for the failure of the Stalinist Lava brothers in their preaching of class war. And, in a later generation, such widespread religiosity also helped reduce the Maoist and neo-Maoist, Jose Ma. Sison, to becoming an exile in northern Europe who plotted long-distance murders.

However similar the ethnolinguistic structures of the Philippines and Indonesia, however analogous the defects of their political economies, their takes on their national histories spin in different religious vortices. Thamrin, who died in a Dutch prison in 1941, and Sudirman, who died of tuberculosis in 1949 after commanding the armies of revolution against the Dutch, are passively remembered by name in the connecting major avenues from the heart of Old Jakarta into the suburbs of the city. But Rizal, for his sacrifice, is venerated by many Filipinos as a nearly, or fully, religious figure. The Filipino commoner, in suffering, is inspired by his national martyrdom, which is often felt to be more intimate and real than the classic Christian passion.

*

The political economies of Phil-Indo are both badly wounded. Each may also be considered as suffering from severe domestic parasitism. In Indonesia, the TNI wages suppressive wars as part of its countrywide business plan. The felt consequence of that, and its unchanged territorial system, gives the critics of TNI ample evidence to say that it behaves like an army of occupation, and that it exploits the nation. In the Philippines, two feelings grow and tend to merge: in class terms, most of the people are felt to be exploited by an educated elite; and with regard to power, the hyphenated term, "nation-state," is felt to signify the colonization of the nation by the state.

All states are fallible; some more than others. All societies are unfinished; and some, more than others, are in need of new beginnings. Religions may be fixed revelations to orthodox believers, but they are supple resources to other seekers. They are modes of considering life above the state and within the society — ways of negotiating realities for the self which are superior to what is offered by priests and imams. Religiosity becomes rejection of the given, and transcendence of the obvious. Religion itself, well-preached and lived well, should minimize the false god of megatrend, and allow living in *metanoia*, for one's share of the sublime. In oppressive societies, however, religion may not do so. Then religiosity may open ways to act with regard to one's deprivations and frustrations.

Perhaps, as in the days of early Christian observance and early Islamic belief, religion is, above all, creative resistance to pagan crudity and to power-brutishness. Forces of Darkness, Desire, Ignorance, and Wrath are always around us. With the aid of religion, human beings struggle against these Powers.[10]

Sometimes, however, organized religion itself seems limiting. When one's social options are constricted, and open political action may be dangerous, then an ultrasocial and intrapolitical life may be necessary; a life of resistance; a life perhaps beleaguered, but relieved by new allegiances; a life of transient ritual, but private immanence and even epiphany. Not passive, not escapist, such a life; but dialogical, oppositional, and determined. Religiosity, in these senses, ranging beyond the church and the mosque, allows the soul, in its contention with the Powers, the possibility of continuous ascent.

---

[10] The capitalized terms are as translated and used (pp. 16, 79-81) in Karen L. King, *The Gospel of Mary of Magdala: Jesus and the First Woman Apostle* (Santa Rose, CA: Polebridge Press, 2003). Dr. King is the Winn Professor of Ecclesiastical History at the Harvard Divinity School.

Fig. 34

Estrada Loyalists at the Supreme Court. Followers of the deposed president had their own concepts of constitutionality and of religiosity. Here they demonstrate in front of the Supreme Court, against the arrest warrant for a populist politician who had first won fame as a cinematic hero defending the poor. (17 April 01, "rah 1," *Philippines Enquirer*)

Fig. 35

"EDSA III." Estrada loyalists carried their protests to the very shrine commemorating the first global spread of the term "people power" in 1986, which had just been rededicated by neo-establishment forces two months earlier in 2001. (see Fig. 33) Signs now displayed, however, such as "Poor is Power," have a totally different flavor. (25 April 01, "ea 11," *Philippines Enquirer*) And actions, including physical defiling of the shrine, jolted the Church, which had thought of itself not only as custodian of public morality, but as a caretaker of the very people now protesting.

Fig. 36

Defending "Erap" Against Anti- Riot Police. When police came to take former President Estrada into custody, loyalists surrounded his home in the suburb of Greenhills to try to protect him. One centrally pictured here suggests the social differences

noted between "EDSA III" and EDSA II. (25 April 01, "eb 6," *Philippines Enquirer*)

A middle-class journalist changed his clothes to march with and observe "EDSA III," and found laboring garb and mass-made Japanese rubber sandals to prevail over white collar dress and shoes. "They smelled," he said to the renowned novelist F. Sionil Jose. Out of his own simple provincial background, Jose reported the remark to the editor with a mixture of sympathy and embarrassment.

Fig. 37

"Suicidal Attack on Malacanang Palace." This front page headline, 30 April 2001, accompanied the photo and details of a march of Erap loyalists culminating in violence, from which six were eventually counted as killed. (Dennis Sabangan, *Philippines Enquirer*) The sequence of happenings called "EDSA III" did not conclusively desacralize the EDSA shrine, which again became a rallying point for middle-class Filipinos against the "Oakwood Mutiny" of young military officers in July 2003. But the twenty-year flow of events, 1986-2005, suggests the inherent instability of sanctifying places and actions which touch class tension in the Philippines, and the nation's continuing political discord.

Fig. 38

Oust Arroyo. Thousands of protestors march, 25 July 2005, and give a thumbs-down sign to President Gloria Macapagal Arroyo. (Jay Directo, AFP, Getty Images) The Philippine House of Representatives subsequently dismissed, by a margin of three to one, impeachment complaints for her interference with the Commission on Elections during the presidential counting, 2004. That did not end the matter. Many Filipinos still looked to judicial remedy from the Supreme Court, or to popular expression of sovereign will in the "parliament of the streets."

The event shown above, on the day of the President's annual state of the nation address, concluded with a burning of her effigy. Arroyo-in-ashes, 2005, contrasts sharply with the exaltation that elevated her to office in 2001 (fig. 33). EDSA I (1986) was of course a more profound historical moment (figs. 19-23). It is clear, however, that phases of high religiosity are not necessarily phenomena of deep religion, and cannot be counted on for enduring political resolution.

About the Authors

Azyumardi Azra is the Rektor of Universitas Islam Negeri in Jakarta, and editor-in-chief of *Studia Islamika*, an Indonesian journal of Islamic studies which he founded in 1993. He is also on the board of editors of the *Journal of Qur'anic Studies*. In the 1990s he held visiting positions at Oxford, the University of the Philippines, Diliman, and Universiti Malaya. His nine books published by the year 2000 include *Renaisans Islam di Asia Tengara* (Renaissance of Islam in Southeast Asia), which won national award as the best book of the year in humanities and social sciences, determined by the Book of Distinction Foundation affiliated with the Ministry of National Education. His latest book is *The Origins of Islamic Reformism in Southeast Asia* (Asian Studies Association of Australia, in association with Allen and Unwin, University of Hawaii Press, and KITLV Leiden, 2004). Azra is Professorial Fellow at the University of Melbourne (2004-09), and a Trustee of the International Islamic University, Islamabad (2004-09). In 2005, Carroll College (Montana) awarded him an honorary doctorate in the humanities; and the Asia Foundation, celebrating its Fiftieth Year, recognized his significant contributions to modernizing Islamic education. In conjunction with commemorating the sixtieth year of Indonesian independence, President Susilo Bambang Yudhoyono awarded him the Bintang Mahaputra Utama, highest award to an Indonesian civilian, for his contributions to the empowerment of moderate and progressive Islam.

Fr. Jose M. Cruz, S.J., is the Dean of the School of Social Sciences, Ateneo de Manila University, in the Philippines. A historian by training, his investigations have mainly been on 17th century Philippines. Among his publications is an edition of Declaración de la doctrina Christiana, Juan de Oliver, OFM (+1599). Father Cruz earned his B.A. from Ateneo de Manila University and his Ph.D. from Cornell University. He chairs the governing board of the Regional Centre for History and Traditions, Southeast Asian Ministers of Education.

Donald K. Emmerson is Professor and Senior Fellow at the Institute for International Studies at Stanford University. He heads the Southeast Asia Forum of the Asia Pacific Research Center, teaches courses in international relations and comparative politics, and co-convenes a monthly seminar on democratization. His current project with the Forum is a national review of US policy choices regarding Indonesia. Writings by Dr. Emmerson have appeared recently in the *Brown Journal of World Affairs*, the *Van Zorge Report on Indonesia*, and *YaleGlobal*, among other periodicals, and in edited volumes such as *Asia Pacific Economic Cooperation, The Asia Pacific in the New Millennium,* and *The Many Faces of Asian Security.* In 2001, Gramedia (Jakarta) published his expansion and translation of an edited volume, *Indonesia Beyond Suharto* (1999). He is a member of the Editorial Board of the *Journal of Democracy,* the Shorenstein Asia Journalism Award Committee, and the Social Science Research Council's East Asia Regional Advisory Panel. Prior to moving to Stanford in 1999, he was a professor of political science and Southeast Asian Studies at the University of Wisconsin-Madison. He received his Ph.D. from Yale University.

Theodore (Dorie) Friend is a Senior Fellow with the Foreign Policy Research Institute, Philadelphia. He is also President Emeritus and Trustee of the Eisenhower Fellowships, where he served as President, 1984-96. He was President of Swarthmore College, 1973-82. He is a member of the Board of Advisors of the United States-Indonesia Society. In 2004, he was C.V. Starr Distinguished Visiting Professor of Southeast Asia Studies at the Johns Hopkins University School of Advanced International Studies (SAIS). Previous positions include: Fellow, Rockefeller Center for Artists and Scholars, Bellagio (1988); Fellow, Woodrow Wilson International Center for Scholars (1983-84); and Guggenheim Fellow, Indonesia, Philippines, and Japan (1967-68). Dr. Friend's books include: *Indonesian Destinies,* Harvard University Press (2003); *The Blue-Eyed Enemy: Japan Against the West in Java and Luzon, 1942-45,* Princeton University Press (1988); *Between Two Empires: The Ordeal of the Philippines, 1929-1946,* Yale University Press (1965); and a novel, *Family Laundry* (1986). Dr. Friend has been a nationally ranked senior squash player for twenty years. His scholarly research interests include cultural issues, democratization, development, foreign relations, modern history, and political economy. He received his Ph.D. in History from Yale University.

Robert W. Hefner is Professor of Anthropology and Associate Director of the Institute for the Study of Economic Culture at Boston University, as well as a Senior Research Scholar on Religion and Democracy at the Institute on Religion and World Affairs. He has written or edited ten books, including *Civil Islam: Muslims and Democratization in Indonesia* and, as editor, *The Politics of Multiculturalism: Pluralism and Citizenship in Malaysia, Singapore, and Indonesia; Democratic Civility: The History and Cross-Cultural Possibility of a Modern Political Ideal; Market Cultures: Society and Morality in the New Asian Capitalisms;* and, with Patricia Horvatich, *Islam in an Era of Nation-States: Politics and Religious Renewal in Muslim Southeast Asia.* Dr. Hefner is currently coordinating a multi-country project with thirteen senior specialists of Islam for the Institute on Religion and World Affairs and the Pew Charitable Trusts entitled, "Civil Democratic Islam: Prospects and Policies for a Changing Muslim World." He also serves as the editor for the sixth volume of the New

Cambridge History of Islam, *Islam and Modernities: Society and Culture in the Muslim World since 1800*. He received his Ph.D. in Anthropology from the University of Michigan.

Vicente Leuterio Rafael is Professor of History at the University of Washington in Seattle, where he also serves as a Fellow at the Simpson Humanities Center. Since 1997, he has also taught at the Ateneo de Manila University, Cornell University, University of Hawaii at Manoa, and the University of California, San Diego. His courses have included communications, anthropology, colonialism, and technology and its impacts on culture. Dr. Rafael has edited two volumes on Indonesia and the Philippines, and has written four books, including the forthcoming work, *The Promise of the Foreign: Translation, Technology and Nationalism in the Spanish Philippines*, from Duke University Press. He received the National Book Award for History from the Manila Critics Circle for his book, *White Love and Other Events in Filipino History* (2000). Dr. Rafael is concurrently a member of the Southeast Asia Council and Harry Benda Prize Committee in the Association for Asian Studies, the editorial board of the journal *Cultural Anthropology*, and the advisory boards of the journals *Positions* and *Public Culture*. He has also served on committees at the Social Science Research Council and the American Council of Learned Societies. Dr. Rafael has been a visiting fellow at the East-West Center, the University of Michigan, the University of California, Irvine, and the Rockefeller Foundation Bellagio Study Center, Bellagio, Italy.

Jose Eliseo (Joel) Rocamora has been Executive Director of the Institute for Popular Democracy in Manila for the past nine years. He is a member of the Executive Committee of Akbayan (Citizens Action Party), on the Advisory Committee for the Institute for Development Studies, University of Sussex, and a columnist for the news magazine "Newsbreak." From 1992 to 1997, he served as a consultant for the Institute for Popular Democracy, Center for Social Policy and Public Affairs at Ateneo University, and for the UNDP on an assessment of a poverty alleviation program and on an assessment of civil society capabilities in Muslim areas in Mindanao. Prior to that, he served as Director for the Philippine Resource Center and as Co-director for the Southeast Asia Resource Center in Berkeley, California. Dr. Rocamora has written and edited nine books, and contributed articles or chapters to many publications. His books include *Nationalism in Search of Ideology: The Indonesian Nationalist Party, 1946-65* (1975) and *Breaking Through: The Struggle Within the Communist Party of the Philippines* (1994), which won the National Book Award of the Manila Critics Circle. Dr. Rocamora received his Ph.D. in Politics, Asian Studies, and International Relations from Cornell University.

David Joel Steinberg has been President of Long Island University, the thirteenth largest private university in the United States, since 1985. He is author of *Philippine Collaboration in World War II*, winner of the University Press Award in 1969; *The Philippines: A Singular and a Plural Place* (now in its fourth edition); and coauthor of *In Search of Southeast Asia*, one of the most widely used textbooks in the field. He has consulted for the Ford Foundation and the United Nations Fund for Population Activities, and has testified before the United States Congress on many occasions. He received his Ph.D. in History from Harvard, and has taught at the University of Michigan and Brandeis University.